PREFACE

1. Scope

This publication provides doctrine for the Armed Forces of the United States when they operate as part of a multinational force. It addresses operational considerations that the commander and staff should consider during the planning and execution of multinational operations.

2. Purpose

This publication has been prepared under the direction of the Chairman of the Joint Chiefs of Staff (CJCS). It sets forth joint doctrine to govern the activities and performance of the Armed Forces of the United States in joint operations and provides the doctrinal basis for US military coordination with other US Government departments and agencies during operations and for US military involvement in multinational operations. It provides military guidance for the exercise of authority by combatant commanders and other joint force commanders (JFCs) and prescribes joint doctrine for operations and training. It provides military guidance for use by the Armed Forces in preparing their appropriate plans. It is not the intent of this publication to restrict the authority of the JFC from organizing the force and executing the mission in a manner the JFC deems most appropriate to ensure unity of effort in the accomplishment of the overall objective.

3. Application

a. Joint doctrine established in this publication applies to the Joint Staff, commanders of combatant commands, subunified commands, joint task forces, subordinate components of these commands, and the Services.

b. The guidance in this publication is authoritative; as such, this doctrine will be followed except when, in the judgment of the commander, exceptional circumstances dictate otherwise. If conflicts arise between the contents of this publication and the contents of Service publications, this publication will take precedence unless the CJCS, normally in coordination with the other members of the Joint Chiefs of Staff, has provided more current and specific guidance. Commanders of forces operating as part of a multinational (alliance or coalition) military command should follow multinational doctrine and procedures ratified by the United States. For doctrine and procedures not ratified by the United States, commanders should evaluate and follow the multinational command's doctrine and procedures, where applicable and consistent with US law, regulations, and doctrine.

For the Chairman of the Joint Chiefs of Staff:

CURTIS M. SCAPARROTTI
Lieutenant General, U.S. Army
Director, Joint Staff

i

Intentionally Blank

• Updates discussion on security cooperation to align with proponent Joint Publication (JP) 3-22, *Foreign Internal Defense*, and JP 1-02, *DOD Dictionary of Military and Associated Terms*.

• Removes and replaces the term "strategic communications" and/or "SC" with "communication synchronization" throughout the JP.

• Utilizes the term "multinational" throughout the document to represent the myriad of terms that could be used to describe the force.

• Deletes the National Security Structure section at the beginning of Chapter II, "Command and Coordination Relationships."

• Replaces the term "psychological operations" throughout the publication with the term "military information support operations" as appropriate, which more accurately reflects and coveys the nature of planned peacetime or combat operations activities, per Secretary of Defense Memorandum dated 3 December 2010.

• Deletes the Strategic Communications section.

• Updates and cleans up graphics and diagrams throughout the JP.

• Removes old Appendix C, "United Nations and Other Intergovernmental Organizations Considerations."

• Adds new Appendix C, "Multinational Interoperability Council."

Intentionally Blank

TABLE OF CONTENTS

APPENDIX

GLOSSARY

FIGURE

Intentionally Blank

- **Presents Fundamentals of Multinational Operations**

- **Identifies Command and Coordination Relationships**

- **Describes Planning and Execution Considerations**

Fundamentals of Multinational Operations

Multinational Operations Overview

Multinational operations are operations conducted by forces of two or more nations, usually undertaken within the structure of a coalition or alliance. Other possible arrangements include supervision by an intergovernmental organization (IGO) such as the United Nations (UN), the North Atlantic Treaty Organization (NATO), or the Organization for Security and Cooperation in Europe. Two primary forms of multinational partnership that the joint force commander (JFC) will encounter are an alliance or a coalition. An alliance is the relationship that results from a formal agreement between two or more nations for broad, long-term objectives that further the common interests of the members. A coalition is an arrangement between two or more nations for common action.

Strategic Context

Nations form partnerships in both regional and worldwide patterns as they seek opportunities to promote their mutual national interests, ensure mutual security against real and perceived threats, conduct foreign humanitarian assistance and disaster relief operations, and engage in peace operations. US commanders should expect to conduct military operations as part of a multinational force (MNF).

Nature of Multinational Operations

While the tenets [of multinational operations] cannot guarantee success, ignoring them may lead to mission failure due to a lack of unity of effort. The tenets are respect, rapport, knowledge of partners, patience, mission focus, and trust and confidence.

Security Cooperation

Security cooperation (SC) involves all Department of Defense (DOD) interactions with foreign defense establishments to build defense relationships that promote specific US security interests, develop allied and friendly military capabilities for self-defense and multinational operations, and provide US forces with peacetime and contingency access to a host nation (HN). Geographic combatant commanders (GCCs) shape their areas of responsibility through SC activities by continually employing military forces to complement and reinforce other instruments of national power. Examples of SC include the National Guard's State Partnership Program, foreign internal defense, and security force assistance.

Rationalization, Standardization, and Interoperability

International rationalization, standardization, and interoperability with friendly nations is important for achieving practical cooperation; efficient use of research, development, procurement, support, and production resources; and effective multinational capability without sacrificing US capabilities. **Rationalization** refers to any action that increases the effectiveness of MNFs through more efficient or effective use of defense resources committed to the MNF. The basic purpose of **standardization** programs is to achieve the closest practical cooperation among multinational partners through the efficient use of resources and the reduction of operational, logistic, communications, technical, and procedural obstacles in multinational military operations. **Interoperability** greatly enhances multinational operations. Nations whose forces are interoperable across material and nonmaterial capabilities can operate together effectively in numerous ways.

Command and Coordination Relationships

Command and Control of United States Forces in Multinational Operations

National command includes the authority and responsibility for organizing, directing, coordinating, controlling, planning employment of, and protecting military forces.

Although nations will often participate in multinational operations, they rarely, if ever, relinquish national command of their forces. As such, forces participating in a multinational operation will always have at least two distinct chains of command: a national chain of command and a multinational chain of command. **As Commander in Chief, the President always retains and cannot relinquish national command authority over US forces.** Command authority for a multinational force commander (MNFC) is normally negotiated between the participating nations and can vary from nation to nation. In making a decision regarding an appropriate command relationship for a multinational military operation, national leaders should carefully consider such factors as mission, nature of the operational environment (OE), size of the proposed US force, risks involved, anticipated duration, and rules of engagement (ROE).

Unified Action

In a multinational environment, unified action synchronizes, coordinates, and/or integrates multinational operations with the operations of other HN and national government agencies, IGOs (e.g., UN), nongovernmental organizations (NGOs), and the private sector in an attempt to achieve unity of effort in the operational area (OA). When working with NATO forces, it can also be referred to as a comprehensive approach.

Multinational Force and Multinational Force Commander

MNFC is a generic term applied to a commander who exercises command authority over a military force composed of elements from two or more nations. The extent of the MNFC's command authority is determined by the participating nations or elements. The MNFC's primary duty is to unify the efforts of the MNF toward common objectives.

Overview of Multinational Command Structures

The basic structures for multinational operations fall into one of three types: integrated, lead nation (LN), or parallel command. A good example of an **integrated command structure** is found in NATO where a strategic commander is designated from a member nation, but the strategic command staff and the commanders and staffs of subordinate commands are of multinational makeup. An **LN structure** exists when all member nations place their forces under the control of one nation. The LN command structure can be distinguished by a dominant LN command and staff arrangement with subordinate elements retaining strict national integrity. Under a **parallel command structure,** no single force commander is designated. The coalition leadership must develop a means for coordination among the participants to attain unity of effort. This can be accomplished through the use of coordination centers.

Multinational Coordination

There are two key structural enhancements that should improve the coordination of MNFs: a liaison network and coordination centers. During multinational operations, US forces should establish liaison early with forces of each nation, fostering a better understanding of mission and tactics, facilitating the ability to integrate and synchronize operations, assisting in the transfer of vital information, enhancing mutual trust, and developing an increased level of teamwork. Another means of increasing MNF coordination is the use of a multinational coordination center. It is a proven means of integrating the participating nations' military forces into the multinational planning and operations processes, enhancing coordination and cooperation, and supporting an open and full interaction within the MNF structure.

Control of Multinational Operations

The degree of control exercised in an MNF is dictated by the MNF structure and the command relationships between members of the MNF. In general, the more centralized the command structure, the greater the MNF's ability to achieve unity of effort.

Interorganizational Coordination

In many operating environments, the MNF interacts with a variety of entities requiring unified actions by the MNFC, including nonmilitary governmental departments and agencies, IGOs, and NGOs. Civil affairs or NATO civil-military cooperation forces enhance interorganizational coordination through the establishment of a civil-military operations center.

Planning and Execution Considerations

Diplomatic and Military Considerations

Any number of different situations could generate the need for a multinational response, from man-made actions (such as interstate aggression) to natural disasters (like an earthquake). In responding to such situations, nations weigh their national interests and then determine if, when, and where they will expend their nation's resources. Nations also choose the manner and extent of their foreign involvement for reasons both known and unknown to other nations. The composition of an MNF may change as partners enter and leave when their respective national objectives change or force contributions reach the limits of their nation's ability to sustain them.

Building and Maintaining a Multinational Force

Building an MNF starts with the political decisions and diplomatic efforts to create a coalition or spur an alliance into action. Discussion and coordination between potential participants will initially seek to sort out basic questions at the national strategic level. The result of these discussions should determine the nature and limits of the response; the command structure of the response force; and the essential strategic guidance for the response force to include military objectives and the desired end states.

Mission Analysis and Assignment of Tasks

Before the multinational task force (MNTF) staff can develop proposed courses of action, the MNFC must conduct an estimate of the situation. This will allow the MNFC to analyze, in an organized manner, the many factors that will affect the accomplishment of the assigned mission(s). This estimate should address the respective capabilities, political will, and national interests of the MNTF components. Based upon these national contributions, and after determining the tasks necessary to achieve the objectives that support mission accomplishment, the MNFC should assign specific tasks to the elements of the MNTF most capable of completing those tasks.

Language, Culture, and Sovereignty

Differing languages within an MNF can present a real challenge to command and control, efficient communications, and unity of effort. Wherever and whenever possible, exchange or liaison officers or nonmilitary translators should be used to facilitate interaction and coordination with HN forces. Commanders should strive to accommodate religious holidays, prayer calls, and other unique cultural traditions important to allies and coalition members, consistent with the situation. Sovereignty issues will be among the most difficult problems the MNFC may be required to mitigate. Often, the MNFC will be required to accomplish the mission through coordination, communication, and consensus, in addition to traditional command concepts. Political sensitivities must be recognized and acknowledged.

Legal

Commanders must ensure that MNTF forces comply with applicable national and international laws during the conduct of all military operations. US forces will comply with the law of war (also referred to as the law of armed conflict) during all armed conflicts and in all other military operations. International agreements are the primary source of rules of international law applicable to US, multinational, and HN forces. The most comprehensive are status-of-forces agreements (SOFAs); however, these may be modified or become inapplicable in time of armed conflict.

Doctrine and Training

When the Armed Forces of the United States participate in multinational operations, US commanders should follow multinational doctrine and procedures that have been ratified by the US. For multinational doctrine and procedures not ratified by the US, commanders should evaluate and follow the multinational command's doctrine and procedures where applicable and consistent with US law, policy, and guidance. When the situation permits, MNFCs at all levels should seek opportunities to improve the contributions of member nation forces through training assistance and resource sharing consistent with agreements between MNF members.

Protection of Personnel, Information, and Critical Assets

Commanders must understand that other nations do not necessarily execute force protection in the same way as the US Armed Forces. US commanders, whether under US control or under a command relationship to an MNF, must continuously assess threats and vulnerabilities while implementing appropriate force protection countermeasures in accordance with published GCC directives.

Rules of Engagement

Obtaining concurrence for ROE from national authorities may be time-consuming but is essential and should begin early in the planning process. Even though the participants may have similar political mandates, ROE may differ among the nations represented. The MNFC should reconcile differences as much as possible to develop and implement simple ROE that can be tailored by member forces to their national policies and law. Complete consensus or standardization of ROE should be sought but may not be achievable.

Combat Identification and Friendly Fire Prevention

Tragically, "fog-of-war" situations can lead to friendly fire incidents. A key survivability enabler, to mitigate friendly fire incidents, is the rapid, reliable identification of friends, foes, and neutrals, also known as combat identification. MNFCs must make every effort to reduce the potential for the unintentional killing or wounding of friendly personnel (to include civilians) by friendly fire.

Intelligence

In most multinational operations, the JFC will be required to share intelligence with foreign military forces and to coordinate receiving intelligence from those forces. A multinational intelligence center is necessary for merging and prioritizing the intelligence requirements from each participating nation and for acquiring and fusing all the nations' intelligence contributions.

Information Sharing

The release of classified information to multinational partners is governed by national disclosure policy (NDP). However, the senior US officer needs to become personally concerned with the issues of intelligence sharing and releasing of information early in the process and clearly state the commander's requirements. Commanders should establish and promulgate clear NDP-compliant guidance to subordinate elements that permit flexibility to share information where and when it is needed.

Communications

Planning considerations include frequency management, equipment compatibility, procedural compatibility, cryptographic and information security, identification friend or foe, and data-link protocols. The MNFC should address the need for integrated communications among all participating forces early in the planning phase of the operation. MNF planning and technical communications systems control centers should be established as soon as possible to coordinate all communications.

Operational Environment

Land Operations. The MNFC may assign the responsibility for land operations to an overall MNF land component commander or a task force (TF) within the MNF command structure. Such TFs may include elements from a single nation or multiple nations depending on the situation and the interoperability factors of the nations involved.

Maritime Operations. In a multinational environment, an operational aim for maritime forces is to exercise sea control or project power ashore; synchronize maritime operations with the other major MNF operational functions of land forces, air forces, and special operations forces (SOF); and support the MNFC's intent and guidance in achieving the MNF mission. Maritime forces are primarily navies; however, they may include maritime-focused air forces, amphibious forces, or other government departments and agencies charged with sovereignty, security, or constabulary functions at sea. Maritime operational responsibility may be assigned to an MNF maritime component commander or a designated TF.

Air Operations. Air operations provide the MNFC with a responsive and flexible means of operational reach. The MNFC can execute deep operations rapidly, striking at decisive points and attacking centers of gravity. Overall MNF air operations will normally be assigned to a multinational force air component commander (MNFACC) (the designation will be based on the type of multinational configuration used in the operation). MNFACC responsibilities include the planning, coordinating, allocating, and tasking of air capabilities/force made available based on the MNFC's air apportionment decision.

Special Operations

SOF can provide specific assistance in the area of assessment, liaison, and training of host country forces within the MNTF OA. Special operations responsibility will normally be assigned to an MNF special operations component commander or to a TF within the MNF command structure.

Joint Fires

Effective fire support coordination in multinational operations may require additional efforts due to differing national priorities and the risk of friendly fire, civilian casualties, and collateral damage. To maximize the fires of the MNF and to minimize the possibility of friendly fire, the MNFC should ensure that fire support coordination throughout the MNF is developed.

Multinational Communications Integration

Multinational communications integration (MCI) is the MNFs' coordination and employment of actions, images, and words to support the achievement of participating nations' overall strategic objectives and end state. MCI consists of coordinated programs, plans, themes, messages, and products synchronized with the actions of all instruments of national power in an MNF at the strategic, operational, and tactical levels.

Multinational Logistics

Successful multinational logistic operations are governed by several unique principles. First, multinational logistic operations are a collective responsibility of participating nations and the MNFC, although nations are inherently responsible for supporting their forces. A second principle is that MNFCs should be given sufficient authority over logistic resources to ensure that the force is supported in the most efficient and effective manner. Third, cooperation and coordination are necessary among participating nations and forces, which should make use of multinational logistic support arrangements in order to reduce the logistic footprint in the OA. Finally, synergy results from the use of multinational integrated logistic support; to ensure this, the MNFC must have visibility of the logistic activity during the operation.

Counterdrug Operations

Counterdrug (CD) operations are inherently interagency and/or multinational in nature. DOD supports the US Government lead agencies for both domestic and international CD operations, so military planning requires coordination and collaboration with relevant agencies and multinational partners.

Personnel Recovery

Personnel recovery (PR) is the sum of military, diplomatic, and civil efforts to prepare for and execute the recovery and reintegration of isolated personnel. PR may occur through three options (diplomatic, civil, or military) or through any combination of these options. In multinational operations, PR does not include noncombatant evacuation operations (NEOs), peacetime search and rescue, or salvage operations.

Host-Nation Support

Host-nation support (HNS) will often be critical to the success of a multinational operation. In general, centralized coordination of HNS planning and execution will help ensure that HNS resources are allocated most effectively to support the MNF's priorities. To assist the MNFC in HNS coordination activities, an HNS coordination cell may be established.

Health Services

The medical assets committed in support of multinational operations consist of health service delivery and force health protection capabilities that span the OE from point of injury/illness to the appropriate role of care. To qualify to participate in the MNF (and for subsequent multinational resourced medical treatment, patient movement, and personal disability compensation), national contingents and individuals allocated or contracted to multinational operations must meet the basic standards of individual health and physical fitness laid down by the surgeon and/or the staff chief medical officer.

Noncombatant Evacuation Operations

NEOs are principally conducted by US forces to evacuate US citizens, but they may be expanded to include citizens from the HN as well as citizens from other countries. In planning for a NEO, the chief of mission, GCC, and JFC may consider the possibility of operating with MNFs. However, the approval for US participation in a multinational NEO will come only from the US President.

Personnel Support

Personnel support for multinational operations remains a national responsibility; however, combatant commanders and subordinate JFCs operating as part of an MNF should establish a SOFA, memorandum of agreement, and/or memorandum of understanding regarding personnel support between members of any alliance and/or coalition prior to the onset of operations that clearly define JFC command authority (operational control, tactical control, etc.) over MNF personnel, command relationships, and reporting channels.

CONCLUSION

This publication provides doctrine for the Armed Forces of the United States when they operate as part of an MNF. It addresses operational considerations that the commander and staff should consider during the planning and execution of multinational operations.

CHAPTER I
FUNDAMENTALS OF MULTINATIONAL OPERATIONS

"Alliances are force multipliers: through multinational cooperation and coordination, the sum of our actions is always greater than if we act alone. We will continue to maintain the capacity to defend our allies against old and new threats. We will also continue to closely consult with our allies as well as newly emerging partners and organizations so that we revitalize and expand our cooperation to achieve common objectives. And we will continue to mutually benefit from the collective security provided by strong alliances."

2010 National Security Strategy

1. Multinational Operations Overview

Multinational operations are operations conducted by forces of two or more nations, usually undertaken within the structure of a coalition or alliance. Other possible arrangements include supervision by an intergovernmental organization (IGO) such as the United Nations (UN), the North Atlantic Treaty Organization (NATO), or the Organization for Security and Cooperation in Europe. Commonly used terms under the multinational rubric include allied, bilateral, coalition, combined, or multilateral. However, within this publication, the term multinational will be used to describe these actions. There are two primary forms of multinational partnership that the joint force commander (JFC) will encounter:

a. An alliance is the relationship that results from a formal agreement between two or more nations for broad, long-term objectives that further the common interests of the members.

b. A coalition is an arrangement between two or more nations for common action. Coalitions are typically ad hoc, formed by different nations, often with different objectives, usually for a single event or for a longer period while addressing a narrow sector of common interest. **Operations conducted with units from two or more coalition members are referred to as coalition operations.**

2. Strategic Context

a. Nations form partnerships in both regional and worldwide patterns as they seek opportunities to promote their mutual national interests, ensure mutual security against real and perceived threats, conduct foreign humanitarian assistance (FHA) and disaster relief operations, and engage in peace operations (PO). Cultural, diplomatic, psychological, economic, technological, and informational factors all influence multinational operations and participation. However, **a nation's decision to employ military capabilities is always a political decision.**

b. US commanders should expect to conduct military operations as part of a multinational force (MNF). These operations could span the range of military operations and require coordination with a variety of US Government (USG) departments and agencies, foreign military forces, local authorities, IGOs, and nongovernmental organizations (NGOs). The move to a more comprehensive approach toward problem solving, particularly in regard to counterinsurgency or stability operations, increases the need for coordination and synchronization among military and nonmilitary entities.

For more information on counterinsurgency and stability operations, see Joint Publication (JP) 3-24, Counterinsurgency Operations, *and JP 3-07,* Stability Operations.

c. Much of the information and guidance provided for unified action and joint operations remains applicable to multinational operations. However, commanders and staffs should account for differences in partners' laws, doctrine, organization, weapons, equipment, terminology, culture, politics, religion, language, and objectives. There is no "standard template" and each alliance or coalition normally develops its own protocols and operation plans (OPLANs) to guide multinational action. However, NATO does have a significant standardization process, in which the US participates, for doctrine and tactics, techniques, and procedures (TTP). Thus US forces operating as an element of a NATO force will comply with NATO Allied joint doctrine ratified by the US.

d. While most partner nations recognize a range of military operations construct similar to that presented in JP 3-0, *Joint Operations* (see Figure I-1), terminology, authorities, level of commitment, and imposed constraints and restraints may not mirror those of US forces. Therefore, JFCs should establish early and continuous liaison to enhance mutual understanding of each MNF's commitment and military limitations (as prescribed by its national law and policy) to facilitate planning and optimize use of each contributing nation's forces.

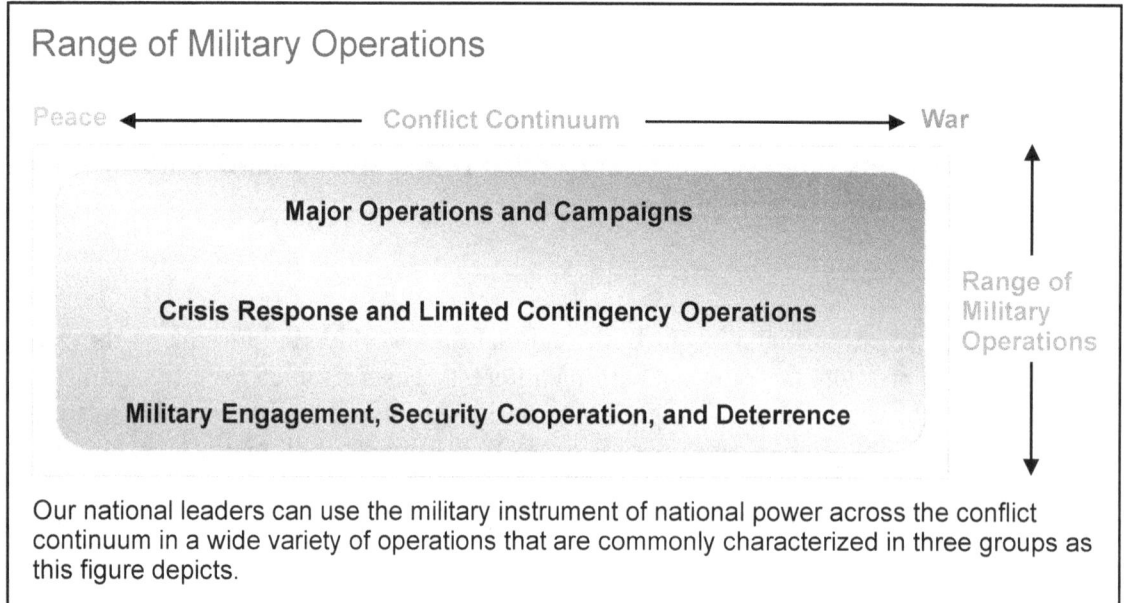

Figure I-1. Range of Military Operations

3. Nature of Multinational Operations

After World War II, General Dwight D. Eisenhower noted that "mutual confidence" is the "one basic thing that will make allied commands work." While the tenets discussed below cannot guarantee success, ignoring them may lead to mission failure due to a lack of unity of effort.

a. **Respect.** In assigning missions and tasks, the commander should consider that national honor and prestige may be as important to a contributing nation as combat capability. All partners must be included in the planning process, and their opinions must be sought in mission assignment. Understanding, discussion, and consideration of partner ideas are essential to building effective relationships, as are respect for each partner's culture, customs, history, and values. Junior officers or even senior enlisted personnel in command of small national contingents may be the senior representatives of their government within the MNF and, as such, should be treated with the courtesy and respect afforded the commanders of other troop contributing nations. Without genuine respect of others, rapport and mutual confidence cannot exist.

b. **Rapport.** US commanders and staffs should establish rapport with their counterparts from partner countries, as well as the multinational force commander (MNFC). This requires personal, direct relationships that only they can develop. When interacting with non-English speakers, knowing at least a few phrases and greetings will help establish a relationship. It is important to remember that eye contact and good listening skills are essential in building rapport. Therefore, when using an interpreter, focus on the person to whom the message is being conveyed. Good rapport between leaders will improve teamwork among their staffs and subordinate commanders and overall unity of effort. The use of liaisons can facilitate the development of rapport by assisting in the staffing of issues to the correct group and in monitoring responses.

c. **Knowledge of Partners.** US commanders and their staffs should have an understanding of each member of the MNF. Much time and effort is spent learning about the enemy; a similar effort is required to understand the doctrine, capabilities, strategic goals, culture, customs, history, and values of each partner. This will facilitate the effective integration of multinational partners into the operation and enhance the synergistic effect of their forces.

d. **Patience.** Effective partnerships take time and attention to develop. Diligent pursuit of a trusting, mutually beneficial relationship with multinational partners requires untiring, evenhanded patience. This is more difficult to accomplish within coalitions than within alliances; however, it is just as necessary. It is therefore imperative that US commanders and their staffs apply appropriate resources, travel, staffing, and time not only to maintain, but also to expand and cultivate multinational relationships. Without patience and continued engagement, established partnerships can easily dissolve.

e. **Mission Focus.** When dealing with other nations, US forces should temper the need for respect, rapport, knowledge, and patience with the requirement to ensure that the necessary tasks are accomplished by those with the capabilities and authorities to accomplish those tasks. This is especially critical in the security line of operation, where failure could prove to have catastrophic results. If operational necessity requires tasks being assigned to personnel who are not proficient in accomplishing those tasks, then the MNF commander must recognize the risks and apply appropriate mitigating measures (e.g., a higher alert level to potential threats).

f. **Trust and Confidence.** Commanders should engage other leaders of the MNF to build personal relationships and develop trust and confidence. Developing these relationships is a conscious collaborative act rather than something that just happens. Commanders build trust through words and actions. Trust and confidence are essential to synergy and harmony, both within the joint force and also with our multinational partners. Coordination and cooperation among organizations are based on trust. Trust is based on personal integrity (sincerity, honesty, and candor). Trust is hard to establish and easy to lose. There can be no unity of effort in the final analysis without mutual trust and confidence. Accordingly, the ability to inspire trust and confidence across national lines is a personal leadership quality to be cultivated. Saying what you mean and doing what you say are fundamental to establishing trust and confidence in a MNF.

4. Security Cooperation

a. Security cooperation (SC) is a key element of global and theater shaping operations and is the means by which the Department of Defense (DOD) encourages and enables countries and organizations to work with the United States to achieve strategic objectives. SC involves all DOD interactions with foreign defense establishments to build defense relationships that promote specific US security interests, develop allied and friendly military capabilities for self-defense and multinational operations, and provide US forces with peacetime and contingency access to a host nation (HN).

b. The *Guidance for Employment of the Force* (GEF) provides the foundation for all DOD interactions with foreign defense establishments and supports the President's National Security Strategy. With respect to SC, the GEF provides guidance on building partner capacity and capability, relationships, and facilitating access (under the premise that the primary entity of foreign engagement is the nation state and the means which geographic combatant commanders [GCCs] influence nation states is through their defense establishments). The GEF outlines SC activities that aim to build partner capacity in the following focus areas: Sustain defense through a partner's human capacity, operational capacity, institutional capacity, civil sector capacity, combined operations capacity, operational access, intelligence sharing, and assuring regional confidence and international collaboration. Additionally, the GEF established processes for assignment, allocation, and apportionment of forces to the GCCs.

c. GCCs shape their areas of responsibility through SC activities by continually employing military forces to complement and reinforce other instruments of national power. The GCC's SC provides a framework within which combatant commands (CCMDs) engage regional partners in cooperative military activities and development. Ideally, SC activities lessen the causes of a potential crisis before a situation deteriorates and requires coercive US military intervention.

d. The GCC's theater campaign plan (TCP) is the primary document that focuses on each command's activities designed to achieve theater strategic end states. The GEF and Joint Strategic Capabilities Plan (JSCP) provide regional focus and SC priorities to the combatant commanders (CCDRs).

e. DOD components develop campaign support plans that focus on activities conducted to support the execution of the GCC's TCP, and on their own SC activities that directly contribute to the campaign end states and/or DOD component programs in support of broader Title 10, United States Code, responsibilities.

For additional information on SC, see Department of Defense Directive (DODD) 5132.03, Department of Defense Policy and Responsibilities Relating to Security Cooperation, the GEF, and the JSCP.

f. The National Guard's State Partnership Program (SPP) establishes enduring relationships between emerging partner nations of strategic value and individual US states and territories. The SPP is an important contribution to the DOD SC programs conducted by the GCCs in conjunction with the National Security Strategy, National Military Strategy, Department of State (DOS), campaign plans, and theater SC cooperation guidance to promote national and CCDR objectives, stability, and partner capacity.

For more detailed discussion on the National Guard SPP, see JP 3-29, Foreign Humanitarian Assistance.

5. Security Cooperation Considerations

a. Foreign internal defense (FID) is the participation by civilian and military agencies of a government in any of the action programs taken by another government or other designated organization, to free and protect its society from subversion, lawlessness, insurgency, terrorism, and other threats to their security. The focus of US FID efforts is to support the HN's internal defense and development, which can be described as the full range of measures taken by a nation to promote its growth and protect itself from the security threats.

b. US military support to FID should focus on assisting an HN in anticipating, precluding, and countering threats or potential threats and addressing the root causes of instability. DOD employs a number of FID tools that interact with foreign defense establishments to build defense relationships that promote specific US security interests, support civil administration, provide nation assistance, develop allied and friendly military capabilities for self-defense and multinational operations, and provide US forces with peacetime and contingency access to an HN. FID typically involves conventional and special forces from multiple Services. Special forces, military information support forces, and civil affairs (CA) personnel are particularly well suited to conduct or support FID.

For additional discussion of FID, see JP 3-22, Foreign Internal Defense.

c. Security force assistance (SFA) is DOD's activities that contribute to a unified action by the USG to support the development of the capacity and capability of foreign security forces (FSF) and their supporting institutions. The US military engages in activities to enhance the capabilities and capacities of a partner nation (or regional security organization) by providing training, equipment, advice, and assistance to those FSF organized under the national ministry of defense (or equivalent regional military or paramilitary forces), while other USG departments and agencies focus on those forces assigned to other ministries (or their equivalents) such as interior, justice, or intelligence services.

d. Successful SFA operations require planning and execution consistent with the following imperatives:

(1) **Understand the Operational Environment (OE).** This includes an awareness of the relationships between the stakeholders within the unified action framework, the HN population, and threats.

(2) **Provide Effective Leadership.** Both MNF and HN leadership must fully comprehend the OE and be prepared, engaged, and supportive in order for the SFA effort to succeed.

(3) **Build Legitimacy.** The ultimate goal of SFA is to develop security forces that contribute to the legitimate governance of the HN population.

(4) **Manage Information.** This encompasses the collection, preparation, analysis, management, application, and dissemination of information.

(5) **Ensure Unity of Effort/Unity of Purpose.** The command relationships must be clearly delineated and understood. Supported and supporting relationships will change over time. Achieving national strategic objectives requires the effective and efficient use of diplomatic, informational, military, and economic instruments of national power supported by interorganizational coordination. A whole-of-government approach integrates the collaborative efforts of the departments and agencies of the USG to achieve unity of effort.

(6) **Sustain the Effort.** This includes two major efforts: the ability of the US/MNF to sustain the SFA effort throughout the campaign, and the ability of the HN security forces to ultimately sustain their operations independently.

For additional discussion of SFA, see JP 3-22, Foreign Internal Defense.

6. **Rationalization, Standardization, and Interoperability**

a. International rationalization, standardization, and interoperability (RSI) with friendly nations is important for achieving practical cooperation; efficient use of research, development, procurement, support, and production resources; and effective multinational capability without sacrificing US capabilities.

b. RSI should be directed at providing capabilities for MNFs to:

(1) Efficiently integrate and synchronize operations using common or compatible doctrine.

(2) Communicate and collaborate at anticipated levels of MNF operations, particularly to prevent friendly fire and protect the exchange of data, information, and intelligence via either printed or electronic media in accordance with (IAW) appropriate security guidelines.

(3) Share consumables consistent with relevant agreements and applicable law.

(4) Care for casualties consistent with relevant agreements and applicable law.

(5) Enhance military effectiveness by harmonizing capabilities of military equipment.

(6) Increase military efficiency through common or compatible Service support and logistics.

(7) Establish overflight and access to foreign territory through streamlined clearance procedures for diplomatic and nondiplomatic personnel.

(8) Assure technical compatibility by developing standards for equipment design, employment, maintenance, and updating so that those nations that are likely to participate are prepared. Extra equipment may be necessary so that non-equipped nations are not excluded. Such compatibility should include secure and nonsecure communications equipment and should address other equipment areas to include (but not limited to): ammunition specifications, truck components, supply parts, and data transmission streams.

Detailed guidance on RSI may be found in Chairman of the Joint Chiefs of Staff Instruction (CJCSI) 2700.01, International Military Agreements for Rationalization, Standardization, and Interoperability (RSI) Between the United States, Its Allies and Other Friendly Nations.

c. **Rationalization.** In the RSI construct, rationalization refers to any action that increases the effectiveness of MNFs through more efficient or effective use of defense resources committed to the MNF. Rationalization includes consolidation, reassignment of national priorities to higher multinational needs, standardization, specialization, mutual support or improved interoperability, and greater cooperation. Rationalization applies to both weapons and materiel resources and non-weapons military matters.

d. **Standardization.** Unity of effort is greatly enhanced through standardization. The basic purpose of standardization programs is to achieve the closest practical cooperation among multinational partners through the efficient use of resources and the reduction of operational, logistic, communications, technical, and procedural obstacles in multinational military operations.

(1) Standardization is a four-level process beginning with efforts for compatibility, continuing with interoperability and interchangeability measures, and culminating with commonality. DOD is actively involved in several multinational standardization programs, including NATO's main standardization fora; the five-nation (US, Australia, Canada, United Kingdom, and New Zealand) Air and Space Interoperability Council (ASIC); the American, British, Canadian, Australian, and New Zealand (ABCA) Armies' Program; and the seven-

nation (Australia, Canada, France, Germany, Italy, United Kingdom, and US) Multinational Interoperability Council (MIC). The US also participates in the five-nation (Australian, Canadian, New Zealand, United Kingdom, and US) Combined Communications-Electronics Board (CCEB) that enables strategic and deployed force headquarters (HQ) information and data exchange, and interoperability of communications-electronics systems above the tactical level of command, and the Australian, Canadian, New Zealand, United Kingdom, United States (AUSCANNZUKUS) Naval command, control, communications, and computers organization working to achieve standardization and interoperability in communications systems.

(2) Alliances provide a forum to work toward standardization of national equipment, doctrine, and TTP. Standardization is not an end in itself, but it does provide a useful framework for commanders and their staffs. Coalitions, however, are by definition created for a single purpose and usually (but not always) for a finite length of time and, as such, are ad hoc arrangements. They may not provide commanders with the same commonality of aim or degree of organizational maturity as alliances.

(3) Alliances usually have developed a degree of standardization with regard to administrative, logistic, and operational procedures. The mechanisms for this standardization are international standardization agreements (ISAs). ISAs can be materiel or nonmateriel in nature. Nonmateriel related ISAs should already be incorporated into US joint and Service doctrine and TTP. The five paragraph operation order is one common example. Materiel ISAs are implemented into the equipment design, development, or adaptation processes to facilitate standardization. In NATO, ISAs are known as standardization agreements (STANAGs) and allied publications (APs) and are instruments that are used to establish commonality in procedures and equipment. The ABCA Standards are another type of ISA. The existence of these ISAs does not mean that they will be automatically used during an alliance's multinational operation. Their use should be clearly specified in the OPLAN or operation order. In addition, these ISAs cannot be used as vehicles for obligating financial resources or transferring resources.

(4) Multinational publications (MPs) are a series of unclassified ISAs specifically developed by NATO. MPs provide signatory nations with common doctrine, TTP, and information for planning and conducting operations. These publications are available to all nations through a NATO sponsor.

(5) Standardization agreements like APs, MPs, STANAGs, and ABCA Standards provide a baseline for cooperation within a coalition. In many parts of the world, these multilateral and other bilateral agreements for standardization between potential coalition members may be in place prior to the formation of the coalition. However, participants may not be immediately familiar with such agreements. The MNFC disseminates ISAs among the MNF or relies on existing standing operating procedures (SOPs) and clearly written, uncomplicated orders. MNFCs should identify where they can best standardize the force and achieve interoperability within the force. This is more difficult to accomplish in coalition operations since participants have not normally been associated prior to the particular contingency. The same considerations apply when non-alliance members participate in an

alliance operation. However, ISAs should be used where possible to standardize procedures and processes.

(6) MNF SOPs provide for standardization of processes and procedures for multinational operations. For example, the Multinational Planning Augmentation Team (MPAT) program developed an MNF SOP with the 31 MPAT nations, has used it within real-world contingencies, and routinely uses it in exercises and training throughout the Asia-Pacific region.

e. **Interoperability.** Interoperability greatly enhances multinational operations. Nations whose forces are interoperable across material and nonmaterial capabilities can operate together effectively in numerous ways. Although frequently identified with technology, important areas of interoperability may include doctrine, procedures, communications, and training.

(1) Factors that enhance interoperability start with understanding the nature of multinational operations as described in paragraph 3, "Nature of Multinational Operations." Additional factors include planning for interoperability and sharing information, the personalities of the commander and staff, visits to assess multinational capabilities, a command atmosphere permitting positive criticism and rewarding the sharing of information, liaison teams, multinational training exercises, and a constant effort to eliminate sources of confusion and misunderstanding. The establishment of standards for assessing the logistic capability of expected participants in a multinational operation should be the first step in achieving logistic interoperability among participants. Such standards should already be established for alliance members.

(2) Factors that inhibit interoperability include restricted access to national proprietary defense information; time available; any refusal to cooperate with partners; differences in military organization, security, language, doctrine, and equipment; level of experience; and conflicting personalities.

Intentionally Blank

CHAPTER II
COMMAND AND COORDINATION RELATIONSHIPS

> *"Even the soldiers of a Democracy cannot always understand the reasons back of strategic situations. Political and military reasons are worked out in cabinets and general staffs and soldiers obey orders."*
>
> **Newton D. Baker, Secretary of State under President Woodrow Wilson**

1. Command and Control of United States Forces in Multinational Operations

Although nations will often participate in multinational operations, they rarely, if ever, relinquish national command of their forces. As such, forces participating in a multinational operation will always have at least two distinct chains of command: a national chain of command and a multinational chain of command (see Figure II-1).

a. **National Command.** As Commander in Chief, the President always retains and cannot relinquish national command authority over US forces. National command includes the authority and responsibility for organizing, directing, coordinating, controlling, planning

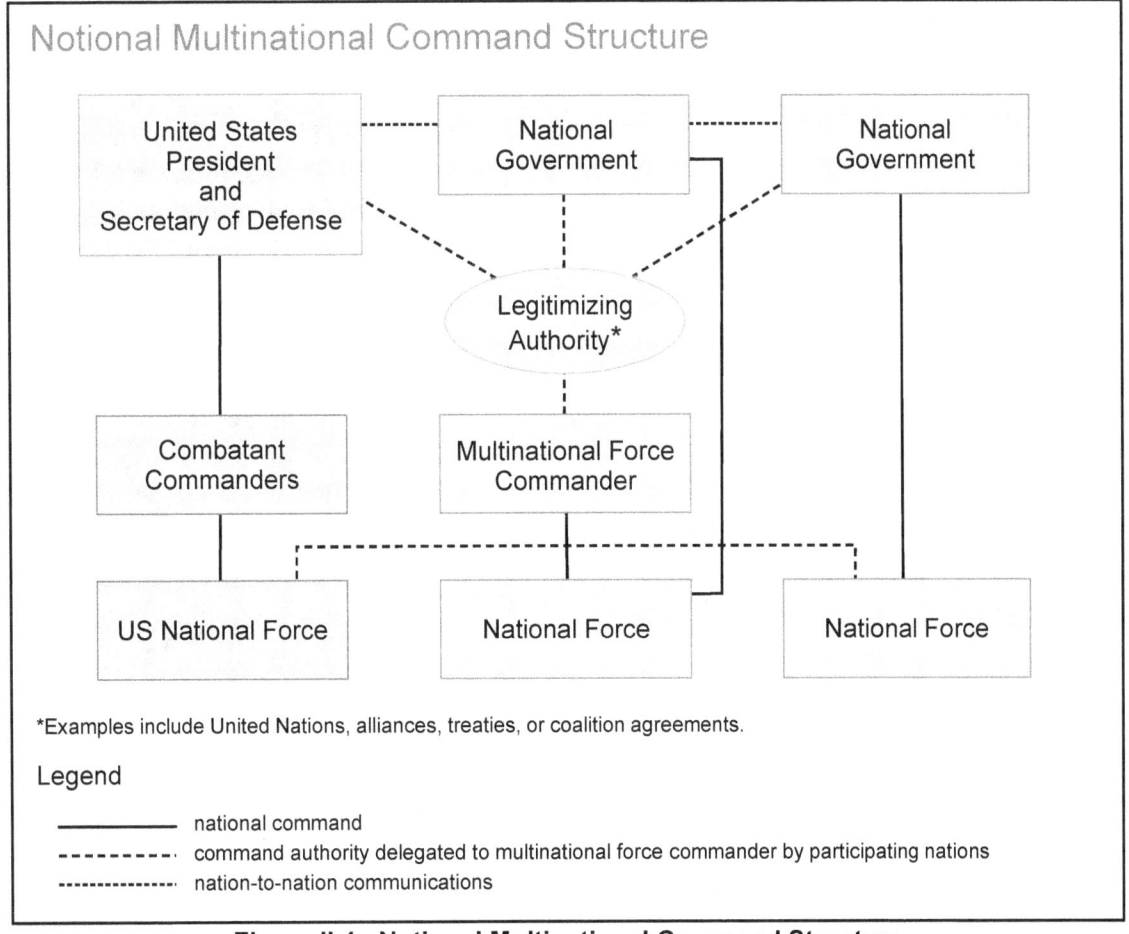

Figure II-1. Notional Multinational Command Structure

COMBINED TASK FORCE (CTF) 151

CTF 151, a multinational task force established to conduct counter-piracy operations in the Gulf of Aden and Somali Basin, operates under a mission-based United Nations Security Council Resolution mandate throughout the Combined Maritime Forces area of operations to actively deter, disrupt and suppress piracy in order to protect global maritime security and secure freedom of navigation for the benefit of all nations. Contributing nations have included ships from Australia, the Republic of Korea, Pakistan, Thailand, Turkey, and the US. In conjunction with the North Atlantic Treaty Organization and European Union Naval Force, ships from CTF 151 patrol in the Somali Basin and the Internationally Recommended Transit Corridor in the Gulf of Aden. CTF 151 also coordinates anti-piracy operations with naval forces from China, Russia, and India.

Various Sources

---

employment of, and protecting military forces. The President also has the authority to terminate US participation in multinational operations at any time.

b. **Multinational Command.** Command authority for an MNFC is normally negotiated between the participating nations and can vary from nation to nation. In making a decision regarding an appropriate command relationship for a multinational military operation, national leaders should carefully consider such factors as mission, nature of the OE, size of the proposed US force, risks involved, anticipated duration, and rules of engagement (ROE). US commanders will maintain the capability to report to higher US military authorities in addition to foreign commanders. For matters that are potentially outside the mandate of the mission to which the President has agreed or illegal under US or international law, US commanders will normally first attempt resolution with the appropriate foreign commander. If issues remain unresolved, the US commanders refer the matters to higher US authorities.

2. Unified Action

a. **Unified action during multinational operations involves the synergistic application of all instruments of national and multinational power;** it includes the actions of nonmilitary organizations as well as military forces. This concept is applicable at all levels of command. In a multinational environment, unified action synchronizes, coordinates, and/or integrates multinational operations with the operations of other HN and national government agencies, IGOs (e.g., UN), NGOs, and the private sector in an attempt to achieve unity of effort in the operational area (OA). When working with NATO forces, it can also be referred to as a comprehensive approach.

b. **Nations do not relinquish their national interests by participating in multinational operations.** This is one of the major characteristics of operating in the multinational environment. Commanders should be prepared to address issues related to legality, mission mandate, and prudence early in the planning process. **In multinational operations, consensus often stems from compromise.**

3. Multinational Force and Multinational Force Commander

a. MNFC is a generic term applied to a commander who exercises command authority over a military force composed of elements from two or more nations. **The extent of the MNFC's command authority is determined by the participating nations or elements.** This authority can vary widely and may be limited by national caveats of those nations participating in the operation. **The MNFC's primary duty is to unify the efforts of the MNF toward common objectives.** An operation could have numerous MNFCs.

(1) MNFCs at the strategic level are analogous to the US GCC level.

(2) MNFCs at the operational level may be referred to as subordinate MNFCs or a multinational task force (MNTF). This level of command is roughly equivalent to the US commander of a subordinate unified command or joint task force (JTF) and is the operational-level portion of the respective MNF. Integrated MNTFs, such as the NATO-led International Security Assistance Force (ISAF), will have embedded MNTF personnel throughout the HQ. Lead nation (LN) MNTF HQ, like Multinational Force–Iraq, will be staffed primarily by LN personnel and augmented by personnel from other MNTF countries. Some integration in staff functions is possible but the bulk of the work will be handled within the LN structure. Figure II-2 illustrates an example of the various command levels.

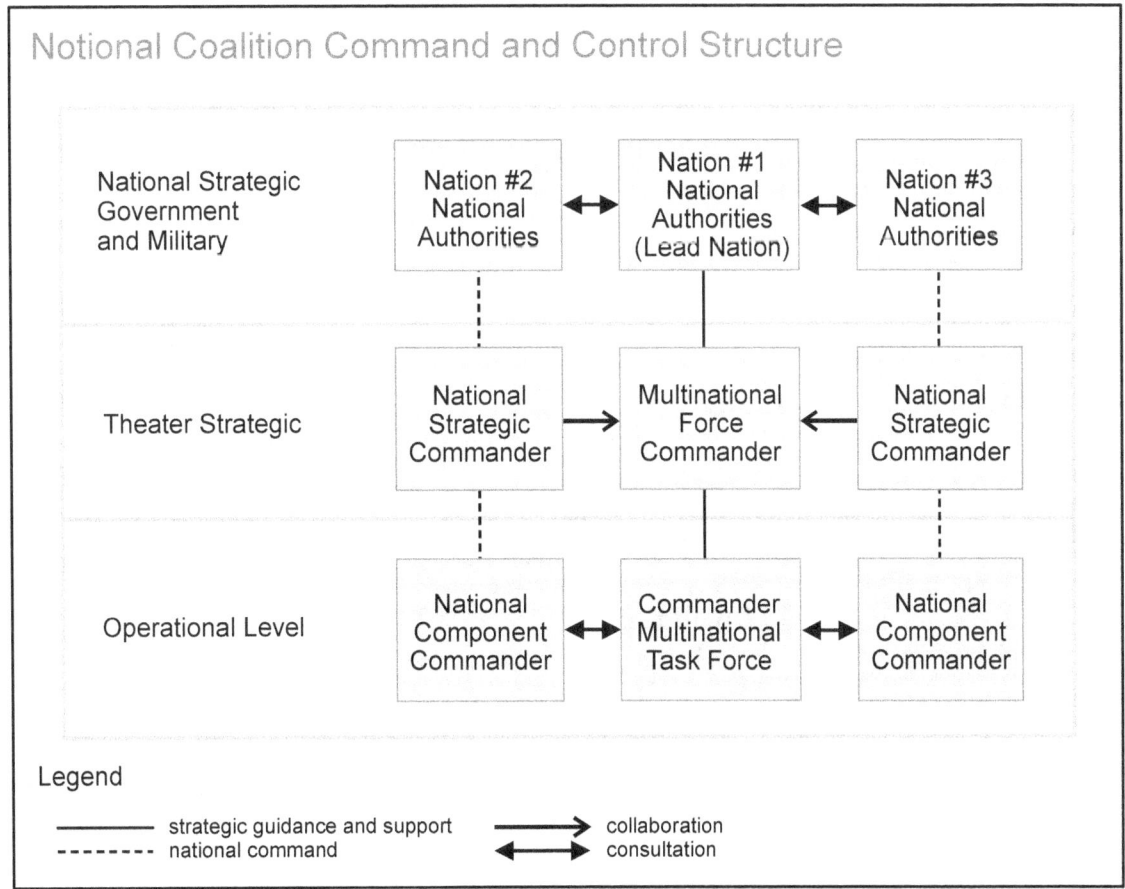

Figure II-2. Notional Coalition Command and Control Structure

b. MNFCs should integrate and synchronize their operations directly with the activities and operations of other military forces and nonmilitary organizations in the OA. All MNTF commanders are responsible to plan and conduct unified actions IAW the guidance and direction received from the national commands, alliance or coalition leadership, and superior commanders.

c. The MNF will attempt to *align* its operations, actions, and activities with NGOs operating in a country or region. NGOs may be precluded from coordinating and integrating their activities with those of an MNF in order to maintain their neutrality.

d. Training of forces within the MNTF command for specific mission standards enhances unified action. The MNFC should consider establishing common training modules or certification training for assigned forces. Such training and certification of forces can occur either prior to or after deployment to the MNTF OA. Certification of forces should be accomplished by a team composed of members from all nations providing military forces to the MNFC.

e. **Nations do not relinquish their national interests by participating in multinational operations.** This is one of the major characteristics of operating in the multinational environment. Commanders should be prepared to address issues related to legality, mission mandate, and prudence early in the planning process. **In multinational operations, consensus often stems from compromise.**

4. Overview of Multinational Command Structures

No single command structure meets the needs of every multinational command, but there is one absolute: political considerations will heavily influence the ultimate shape of the command structure. However, participating nations should strive to achieve unity of command for the operation to the maximum extent possible, with missions, tasks, responsibilities, and authorities clearly defined and understood by all participants. While command relationships are fairly well defined in US doctrine, they are not necessarily part of the doctrinal lexicon of nations with which the US may operate in multinational operations.

a. **Organizational Structure.** The basic structures for multinational operations fall into one of three types: integrated, LN, or parallel command.

(1) **Integrated Command Structure.** A good example of this command structure (see Figure II-3) is found in NATO where a strategic commander is designated from a member nation, but the strategic command staff and the commanders and staffs of subordinate commands are of multinational makeup. The key factors in an integrated command are:

(a) A designated single commander.

(b) A staff composed of representatives from all member nations.

(c) Subordinate commands and staffs integrated into the lowest echelon necessary to accomplish the mission.

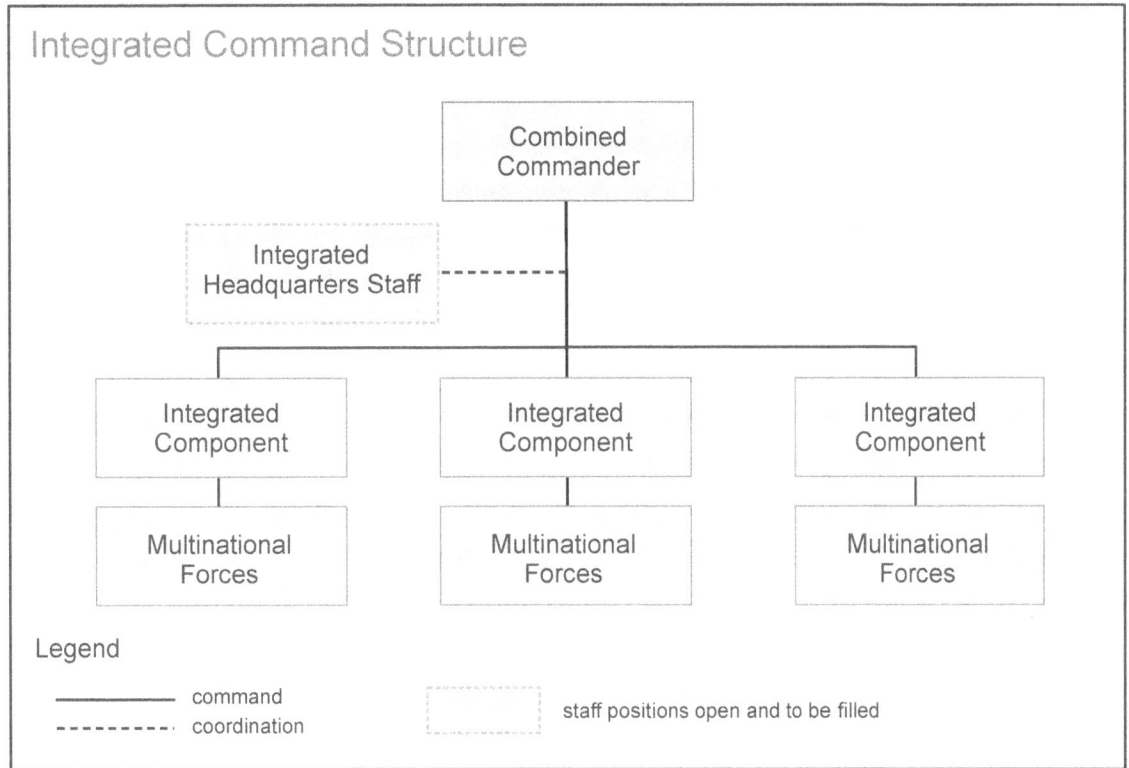

Figure II-3. Integrated Command Structure

(2) **LN Command Structure.** An LN structure exists when all member nations place their forces under the control of one nation (see Figure II-4). The LN command structure can be distinguished by a dominant LN command and staff arrangement with subordinate elements retaining strict national integrity. A good example of the LN structure is Multinational Force–Iraq, wherein a US-led HQ provided overall military command and control (C2) over US and multinational subordinate commands.

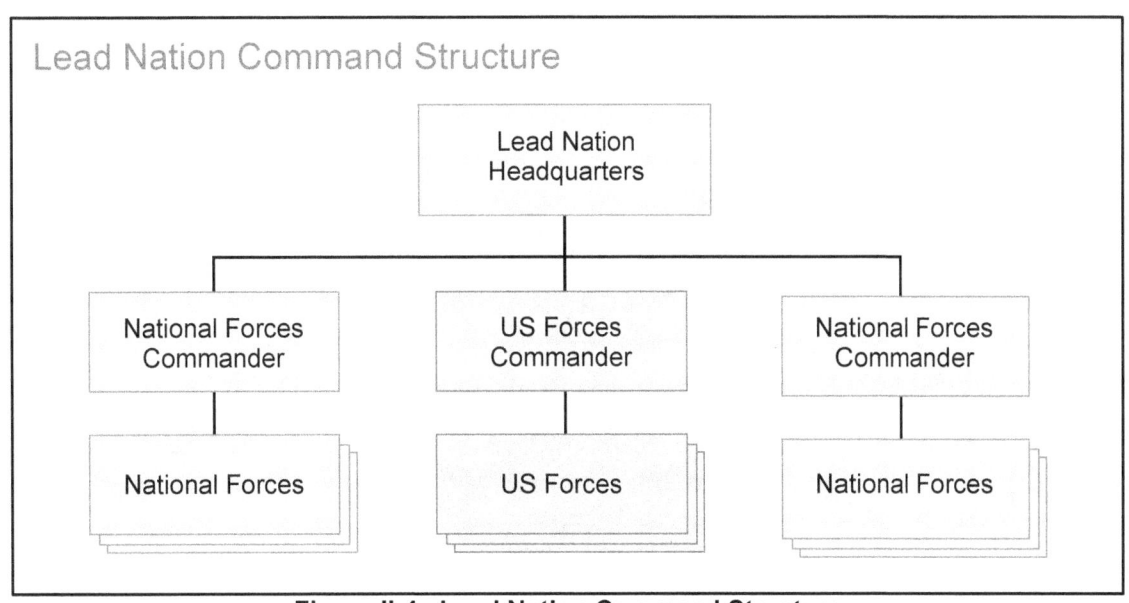

Figure II-4. Lead Nation Command Structure

(a) An LN command structure may also be characterized by an integrated staff and multinational subordinate forces. Integrating the staff allows the commander to draw upon the expertise of multinational partners in areas where the LN may have less experience.

(b) Rotational command, a variation of LN command sometimes found in combined commands, allows each participating nation to be the LN in turn. To be effective, command tour lengths should be adjusted so that participating nations may alternate exercising the authority of the LN. An example of this type of command is the ISAF, which has 12- to 24-month command tours that rotate between the participants.

(3) **Parallel Command Structures.** Under a parallel command structure, no single force commander is designated (see Figure II-5). The coalition leadership must develop a means for coordination among the participants to attain unity of effort. This can be accomplished through the use of coordination centers (see paragraph 8c, "Coordination Centers"). Nonetheless, because of the absence of a single commander, the use of a parallel command structure should be avoided if at all possible.

b. Regardless of how the MNF is organized operationally, each nation furnishing forces normally establishes a national component, often called a national command element, to effectively administer its forces. The national component provides a means to administer and support the national forces, coordinate communication to the parent nation, tender national military views and recommendations directly to the multinational commander, and facilitate the assignment and reassignment of national forces to subordinate operational multinational organizations. In an administrative role, these national components are similar to a Service component command at the unified command level in a US joint organization. The logistic support element of this component is also referred to as the national support

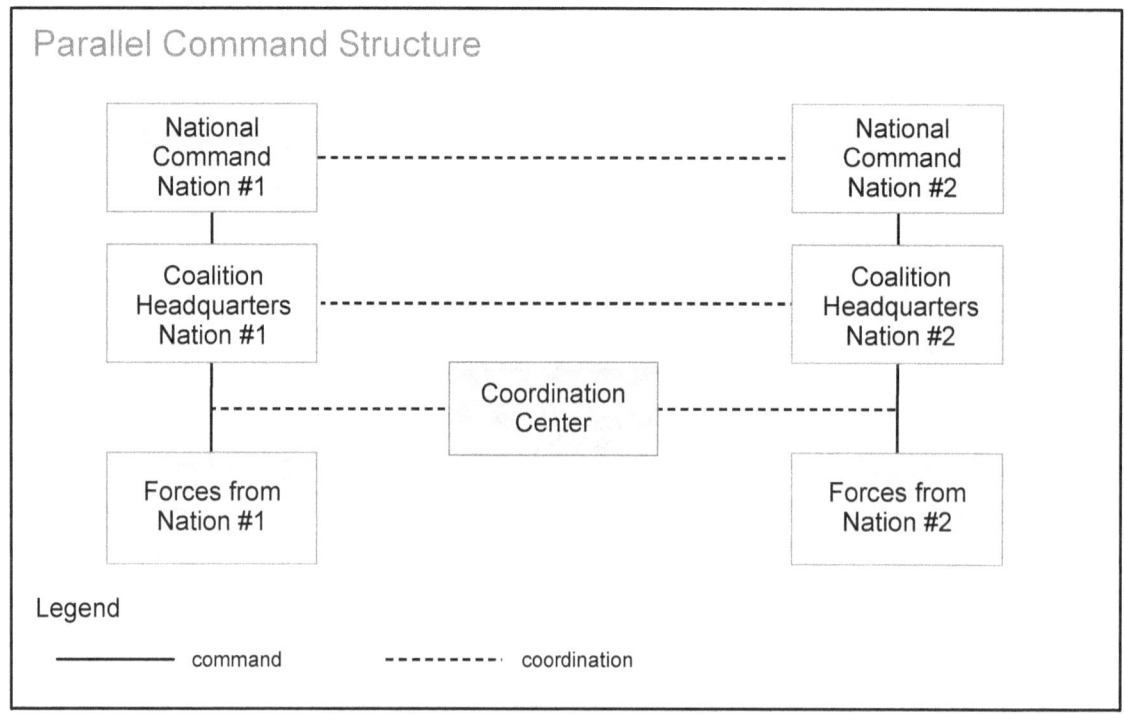

Figure II-5. Parallel Command Structure

element. A national support element may provide common-user logistics support to MNFs as well as national forces. It is also possible that in some operations, selected common-user logistics would be arranged by the multinational joint logistics center (or equivalent), thereby reducing the role of the national support element in providing such logistics.

For additional information on multinational logistic support, see JP 4-08, Logistics in Support of Multinational Operations.

5. Multinational Command Structures

a. In multinational commands, national political objectives are addressed and generally subsumed within MNF objectives at the alliance treaty level. Typically, alliance command structures have been carefully developed over extended periods of time and have a high degree of stability and consensus; doctrine and standardization characterize alliances. Established command structures may be modified or tailored for particular operations, especially when combined operations include non-allied members.

b. Multinational command relationships often reflect either an integrated command structure or an LN command structure. Alliances typically have established command structures, support systems, and standardized procedures. In combined operations, such structures should be used to the maximum practical extent. Combined command and force structures often mirror the degree of allied member participation. Subordinate commands are often led by senior military officers from member nations. Effective operations within an alliance require that the senior political and military authorities be in agreement on the type of command relationships that will govern the operations of the forces. Notwithstanding peacetime command relationships, the political sensitivities associated with actual operations will impact command relationships and operating procedures.

c. Coalitions often form in response to crises that occur outside the area or scope of an established alliance or when the response requires more than an alliance can handle. Coalition command relationships, which evolve as a coalition develops, are most often characterized by one of two basic structures: LN or parallel. In coalition operations, member nations may initially desire to retain even more control of their own national forces than is generally associated with combined operations. At the outset of a coalition, nations are often reluctant to grant extensive control over their forces to one LN. Coalition counterparts are also sensitive to actions that might be construed as preferential to the LN's interests.

d. One means of ensuring that the HQ is representative of the entire coalition is to augment the HQ staff with representatives from the participating coalition members, such as designated deputies or assistant commanders, planners, and logisticians. This provides the coalition commander with representative leadership and a ready source of expertise on the capabilities of the respective coalition members, and facilitates the planning process.

e. During formation of the coalition, the early integration of the multinational national command elements into the coalition planning process can greatly accelerate building of unity of effort and reinforce the tenets of multinational operations. National command elements represent the national command channels from each individual nation within the multinational command. Meetings with the MNFC provide the setting for open, candid input from participating nations.

f. LN and parallel command structures can exist simultaneously within a coalition. This situation occurs when two or more nations or organizations serve as controlling elements for a mix of international forces. The command arrangement used by the Gulf War coalition (see Figure II-6) provides a good example of the intricate web of command structures possible. In that case, the US performed as the LN for a coalition of non-Arab countries while Saudi Arabia functioned as the LN for the Arab coalition members. A friendly forces coordinating council (since renamed to coalition coordination center [CCC]) provided the coordination conduit between the non-Arab (US-led) forces and the Arab/Islamic (Saudi-led) command structures. Terms in the figure reflect the terminology used in the operation.

g. Figures II-7 through II-10 show examples of coalition command structures from Afghanistan ISAF (Figures II-7 and II-8), the NATO Balkans Stabilization Force (Figure II-9), and the Balkans European Force Command (Figure II-10). In the Balkans, when the European Union (EU) assumed the mission from NATO, NATO continued to maintain a military HQ and a place in the command chain as well, with a continued US presence in the country. These diagrams highlight the evolution of multinational command structures, especially those involving IGO such as NATO, the EU, or the UN. These organizations add a layer of complexity to the command structure as nations have to answer to both the IGO chain of command as well as their national political leadership.

6. Multinational Coordination

There are two key structural enhancements that should improve the coordination of MNFs: a liaison network and coordination centers.

a. **Liaison Network.** Effective liaison is vital in any MNF. Differences in doctrine, organization, equipment, training, and national law demand a robust liaison structure to facilitate operations. Not only is the use of liaison an invaluable confidence-building tool, but it is also a significant source of information for the MNFC. During multinational operations, US forces should establish liaison early with forces of each nation, fostering a better understanding of mission and tactics, facilitating the ability to integrate and synchronize operations, assisting in the transfer of vital information, enhancing mutual trust, and developing an increased level of teamwork.

(1) Liaison is often accomplished through the use of liaison teams. These teams should be knowledgeable about the structure, capabilities, weapons systems, logistics, communication systems, and planning methods that are employed within their commands. Liaison requirements for US forces participating in multinational operations are usually greater than anticipated or staffed. Personnel liaison requirements should be identified early during the planning process and staffed accordingly. Team members should be language qualified or provided linguist support. Although professional knowledge and functional expertise are key factors to successful liaison operations, understanding language and culture are equally important and influential.

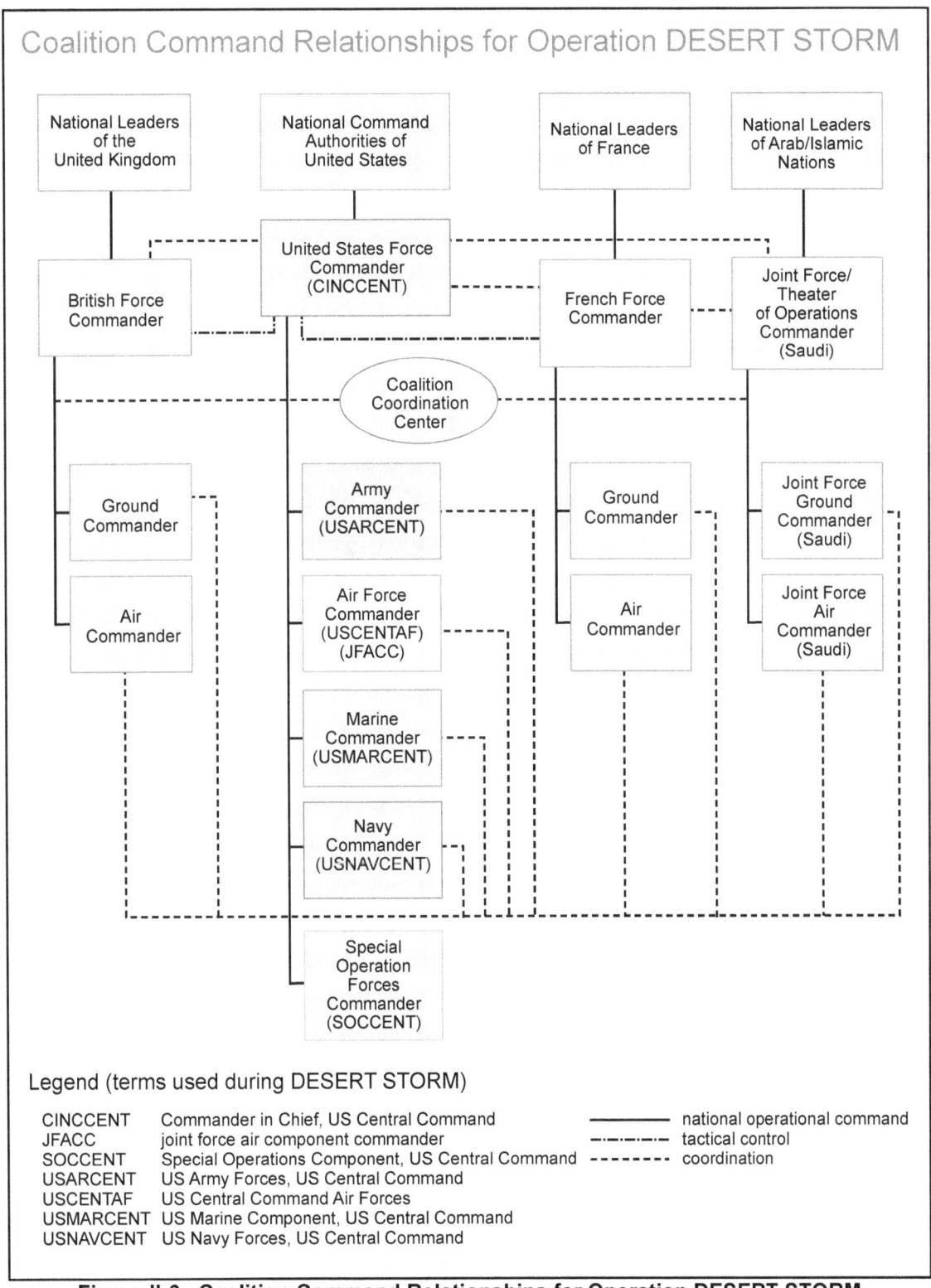

Figure II-6. Coalition Command Relationships for Operation DESERT STORM

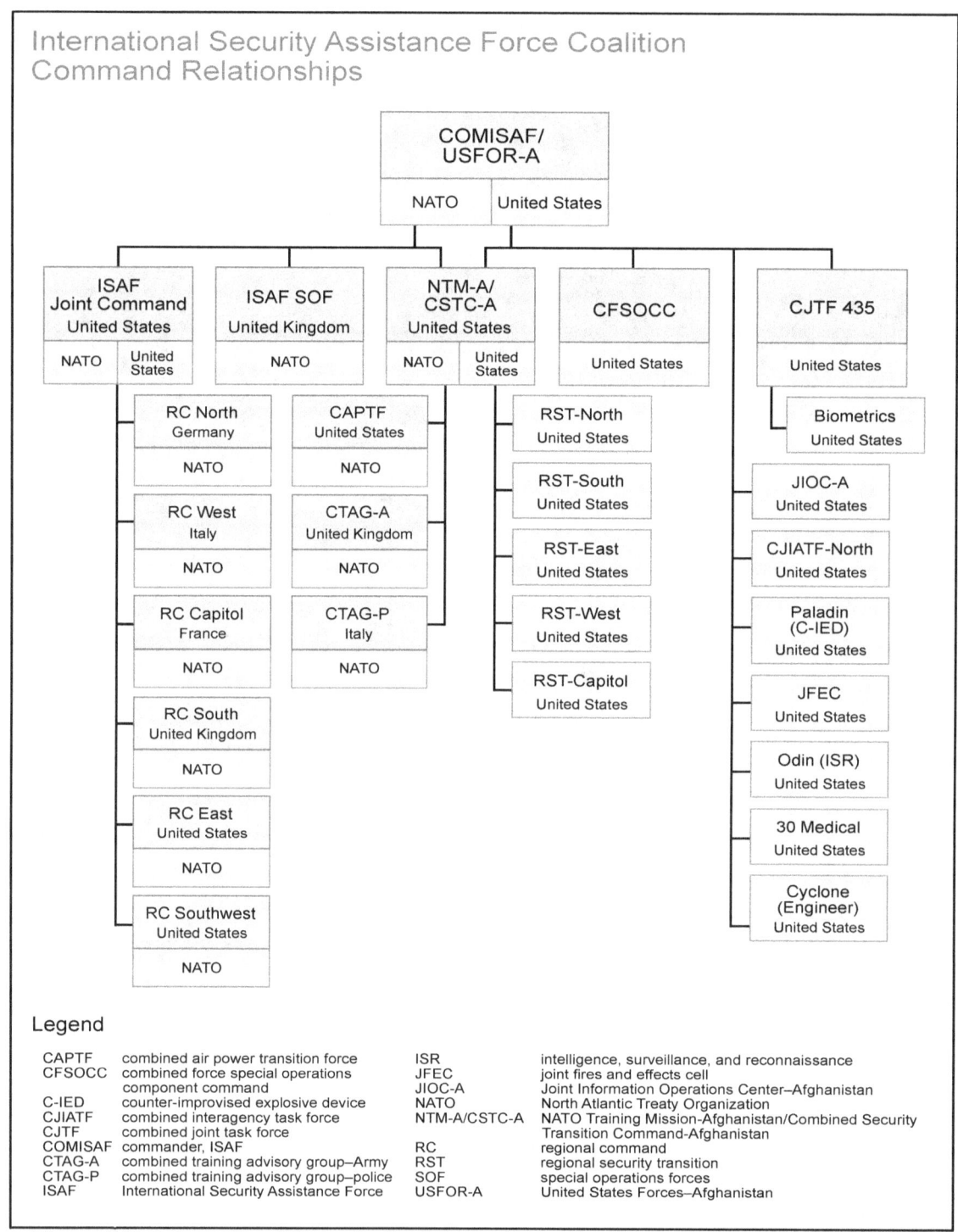

Figure II-7. International Security Assistance Force Coalition Command Relationships

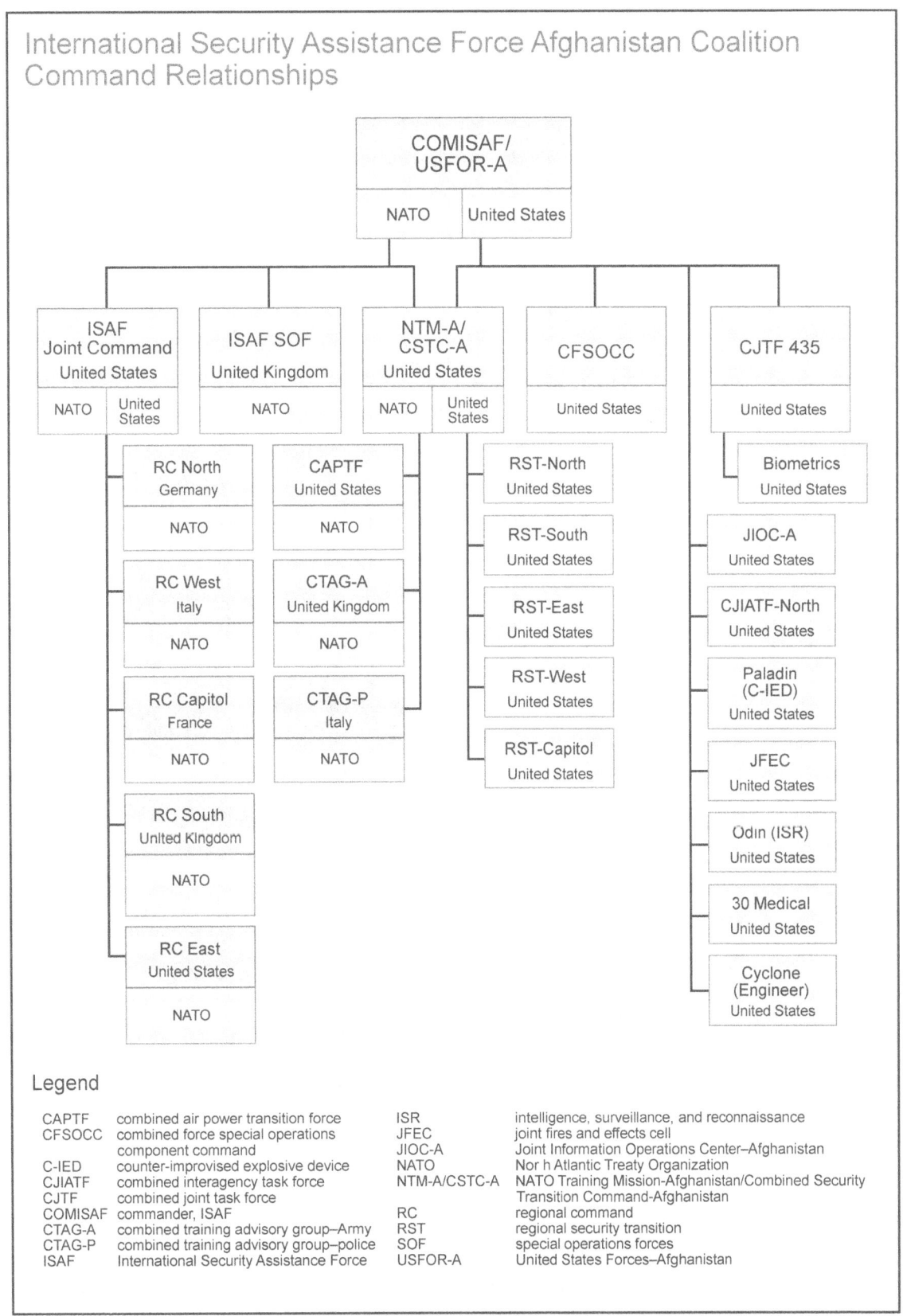

Figure II-8. International Security Assistance Force Afghanistan Coalition Command Relationships

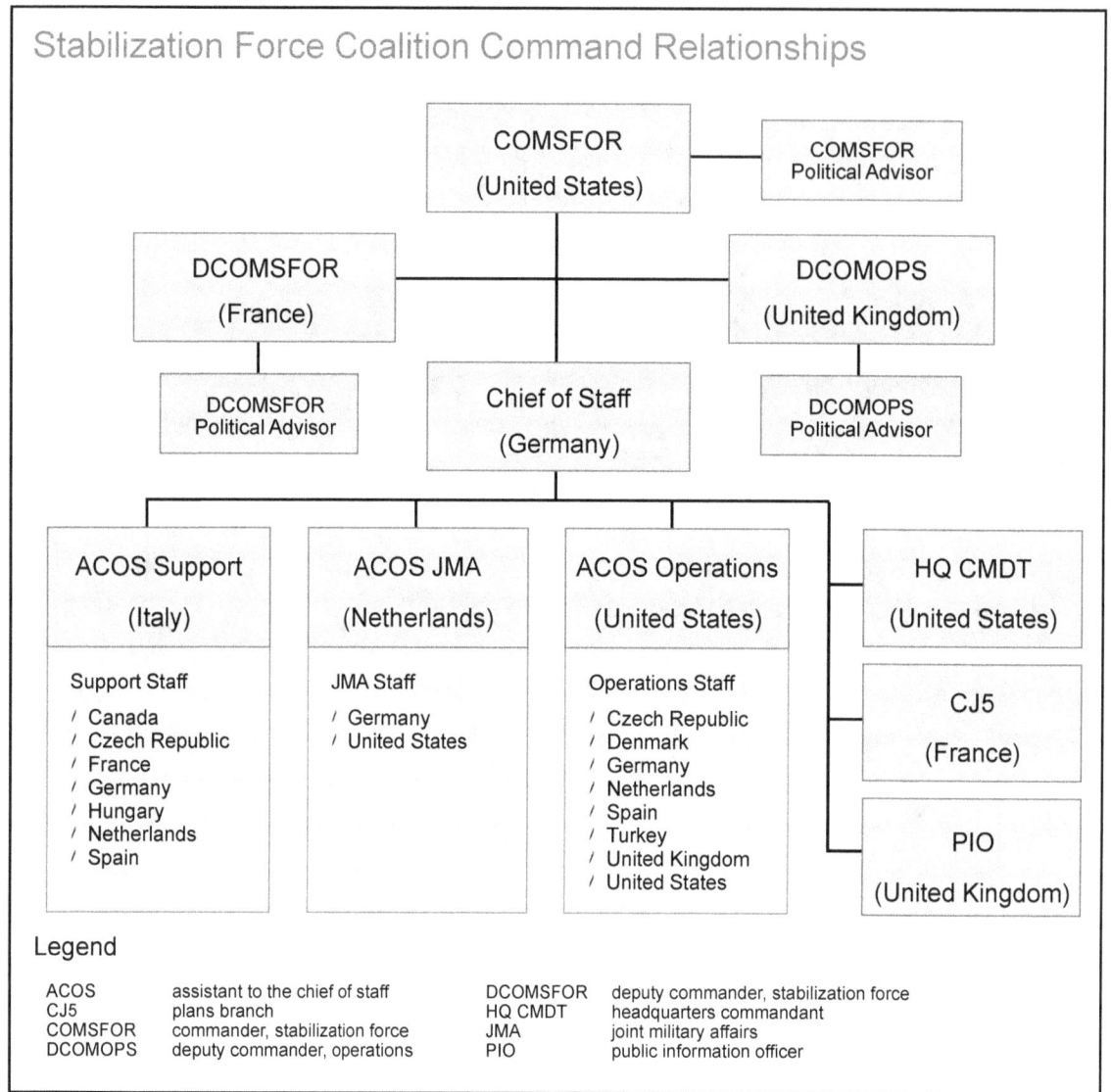

Figure II-9. Stabilization Force Coalition Command Relationships

(2) The US Army's digital liaison detachments (DLDs) have been in existence since Operation DESERT STORM and were used extensively during Operation ENDURING FREEDOM and Operation IRAQI FREEDOM. DLDs are specifically designed to provide US staffs with liaison teams composed of individuals with professional knowledge and functional expertise in associated Army battle command systems to enable interface with multinational units.

For additional information on DLDs, see Army Tactics, Techniques, and Procedures 3-93.2, Digital Liaison Detachments.

(3) Special operations forces (SOF), in conjunction with conventional forces, have proven particularly effective in integrating MNFs. Their language capabilities, regional expertise, cultural awareness, and experience in working and training with other countries'

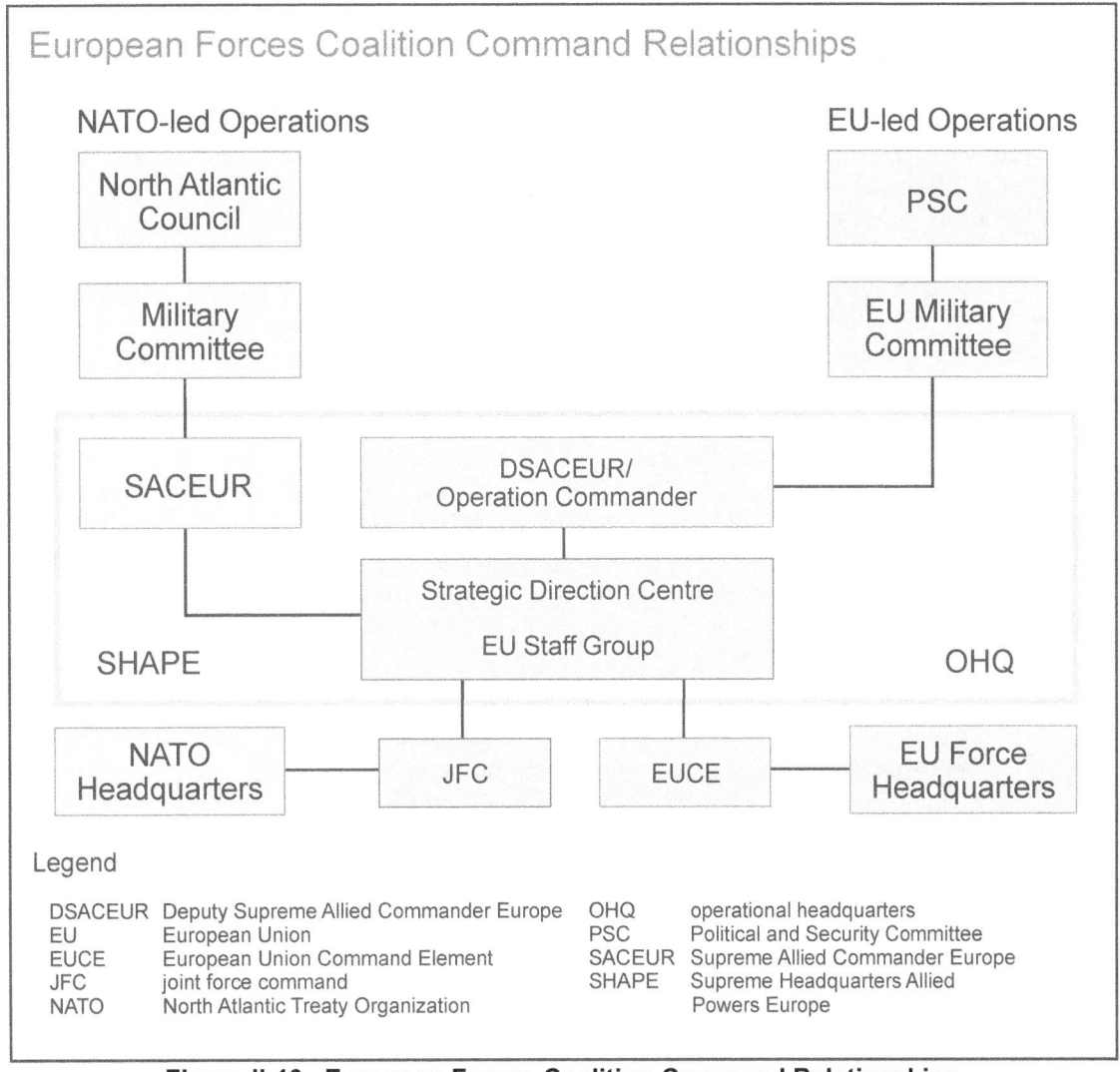

Figure II-10. European Forces Coalition Command Relationships

militaries typically allow them to improve coordination and minimize misunderstanding during MNF operations. Specifically, SOF can assist the MNFC to:

(a) Facilitate the transfer of US defense articles and services under the security assistance program to eligible foreign government military units engaged in internal defense and development operations.

(b) Assess foreign military force capabilities and provide direction or recommendations toward improving HN air-, land-, and sea-power special operations employment and sustainment methods.

(c) Educate foreign military force senior officers and civilians in how to appropriately use special operations military power.

(d) Train foreign military forces to operate and sustain indigenous air/land/sea special operations resources and capabilities.

144TH ARMY LIAISON TEAM DURING OPERATION ENDURING FREEDOM

The 144th Army Liaison Team (ALT) was the third liaison team in this theater of operations. In this theater, the ALT provided liaison to the International Security Assistance Force (ISAF). In accordance with the Bonn Accord, the North Atlantic Treaty Organization (NATO) organized ISAF to support Afghanistan with security and stabilization operations. The 144th ALT arrived in theater and was assigned to Combined Forces Command-Afghanistan at ISAF headquarters. The ALT also provided liaison services primarily for the combined joint operations directorate and the combined joint intelligence directorate, but expanded mission requirements to provide service for all staff sections within the command as required. The 144th ALT provided "air gap" bridging capability for the US SECRET Internet Protocol Router Network, ISAF Secret, the NATO SECRET Crisis Response Operations in NATO Operating Systems, and the Combined Enterprise Regional Information Exchange System (CENTRIXS) which was the coalition network solution. Information security standardization delayed CENTRIXS implementation, as nations were reluctant to share information.

Various Sources

(e) Advise foreign military forces and governmental agencies on how to employ air/land/sea forces in specific operation situations.

(f) Facilitate force integration for multinational operations.

(g) Provide direct support to host countries by using air/land/sea resources to provide intelligence, communications capability, and air or aviation support.

b. **Coordination Centers.** Another means of increasing MNF coordination is the use of a multinational coordination center (MNCC). US commanders should routinely advocate creation of such a center in the early stages of any multinational effort, especially one that is operating under a parallel command structure. It is a proven means of integrating the participating nations' military forces into the multinational planning and operations processes, enhancing coordination and cooperation, and supporting an open and full interaction within the MNF structure. Normally, the MNCC is focused upon coordination of MNF operations, which will most likely involve classified information. The addition of a civil-military operations center (CMOC) is recommended for coordination with the international humanitarian community (IHC). Additional coordination centers may be established to coordinate multinational logistics, functional areas, and media affairs.

(1) Initially, a coordination center can be the focal point for support issues such as force sustainment, alert and warning, host-nation support (HNS), movement control, and training. However, as an MNF matures, the role of the coordination center can be expanded to include command activities.

(2) When a coordination center is activated, member nations provide a staff element to the center that is comprised of action officers who are familiar with support activities such as those listed above. MNF nations should be encouraged to augment this

staff with linguists and requisite communications capabilities to maintain contact with their parent HQ. Apart from a central MNCC such as the CCC, a number of functional coordination centers may also be established within an overall combined logistics coordination or support command for a multinational operation. Activities centrally coordinated or controlled by such centers would include movement control, centralized operational contract support, theater-level logistic support operations, overall medical support, and infrastructure engineering. One key to the success of such centers is the early establishment and staffing with functionally skilled personnel to exercise appropriate control of designated activities.

For additional guidance on organizing and manning an MNCC, refer to the Multinational Planning Augmentation Team (MPAT) Multinational Force (MNF) Standing Operating Procedures (SOP). The MNF SOP can be viewed and downloaded from: https://community.apan.org/mpat/p/sop.aspx.

7. Control of Multinational Operations

The degree of control exercised in an MNF is dictated by the MNF structure and the command relationships between members of the MNF. In general, the more centralized the command structure, the greater the MNF's ability to achieve unity of effort. Integrated command structures, operating within their alliance framework, afford the greatest degree of control. A parallel structure, with its separate lines of command, typically offers the least control and ability to achieve unity of effort. LN structures can exhibit a wide range of control depending on the command relationships assigned.

8. Interorganizational Coordination

a. In many operating environments, the MNF interacts with a variety of entities requiring unified actions by the MNFC, including nonmilitary governmental departments and agencies, IGOs, and NGOs. These groups play an important role in providing support to HNs. Additionally, the MNF should be aware of private sector firms (e.g., businesses, contractors working for the military) operating in the OA. Though differences may exist between military forces and civilian agencies, short-term objectives are frequently very similar. CA or NATO civil-military cooperation (CIMIC) forces enhance interorganizational coordination through the establishment of a CMOC.

b. **Relationships.** The MNFC's relationship with these organizations will vary depending on the nature of the contingency and the particular type of organization involved.

(1) Relationships with other governmental agencies (US and multinational partners) and IGOs should be clearly defined in order to achieve coherent coordination. It is important that interorganizational relationships be clearly defined with respect to required military support before commencement of operations, if possible. In some cases, other agencies may be lead agent for operations with military forces providing support. In other cases, the lead agency is prescribed by law or regulation, or by agreement between allied and coalition forces and the agencies involved. The President, normally through the Secretary of

Defense (SecDef), should provide clear guidance regarding the relationships between US military commanders and USG departments and agencies.

(2) To achieve the greatest unity of effort, the roles, missions, efforts, and activities of the IHC within the MNF OA should be factored into the commander's mission analysis. The MNFC should use coordination tools and appropriate agency/command representatives to enhance planning. Every effort should be made to formally include interorganizational coordination factors and requirements in MNF OPLANs.

(3) In addition, the OPLAN should provide guidance to the MNFC regarding relationships with and support to NGOs and IGOs operating within the OA. Because these organizations do not operate within the military or governmental hierarchy, the relationship between an MNFC, NGOs, and IGOs is neither supported nor supporting. An association or partnership may more accurately describe the relationship that exists between them. Communicating clearly, recognizing each other's limitations, and building consensus and cooperation are critical stepping stones to achieving a unified effort. A transition plan is essential when relieving, replacing, or relinquishing control to NGOs and IGOs. This must begin as early as possible in the planning cycle for such operations. Civil-military operations (CMO) planners should include IGO/NGO capabilities, limitations, and operations within the MNF's plan whenever possible.

c. **Coordination Centers.** MNFCs can achieve significant positive results in accomplishing their missions and shaping better conditions by finding positive ways to interact with these organizations. One means of enhancing the working relationship between NGOs/IGOs when there is no command relationship is through their integration with existing coordination centers, as described in subparagraph 6b, "Coordination Centers." It is possible to operate through a process of cooperation, communication, consensus, collaboration, and coordination to achieve mutual interests. The CMOC can be useful in deconflicting and coordinating operations among these groups, ensuring unity of effort.

For additional information, see JP 3-57, Civil-Military Operations.

d. **Agreements.** The US DOS leads USG negotiations with IGOs and other nations' agencies. Although Congress has tightly restricted the delegation of authority to negotiate and sign agreements with foreign nations, forces, and agencies to DOS, the interagency environment permits establishing formal agreements between the US military and US civilian government agencies. Such agreements can take the form of memoranda of understanding (MOUs) or terms of reference. When appropriate, heads of agencies and military commanders negotiate and cosign plans. Concluding these negotiations prior to the commencement of operations offers the best chance for success. There are regulatory and statutory fiscal constraints involving agreements between the Armed Forces of the United States and other US governmental and nongovernmental departments and agencies. A staff judge advocate (SJA) should be consulted before negotiating or entering into any agreements outside DOD.

For more detailed information on interagency coordination and on agencies expected to be involved, see JP 3-08, Interorganizational Coordination During Joint Operations.

For more information on multinational operations associated with homeland defense and civil support, see JP 3-27, Homeland Defense, *and JP 3-28,* Defense Support of Civil Authorities.

Presidential Policy Directive-1, Organization of the National Security Council System, *provides that the management of the development and implementation of national security policies by multiple agencies of the USG shall usually be accomplished by National Security Council Interagency Policy Committees.*

National Security Presidential Directive (NSPD)-44, Management of Interagency Efforts Concerning Reconstruction and Stabilization, *establishes that the Secretary of State "shall coordinate and lead integrated United States Government efforts, involving all US departments and agencies with relevant capabilities, to prepare, plan for, and conduct stabilization and reconstruction efforts."*

Intentionally Blank

CHAPTER III
PLANNING AND EXECUTION CONSIDERATIONS

> *"There is only one thing worse than fighting with allies and that is fighting without them."*
>
> **Sir Winston Churchill, 1 April 1945**

SECTION A. GENERAL CONSIDERATIONS

1. Diplomatic and Military Considerations

a. Any number of different situations could generate the need for a multinational response, from man-made actions (such as interstate aggression) to natural disasters (like an earthquake). In responding to such situations, nations weigh their national interests and then determine if, when, and where they will expend their nation's resources. Nations also choose the manner and extent of their foreign involvement for reasons both known and unknown to other nations. The composition of an MNF may change as partners enter and leave when their respective national objectives change or force contributions reach the limits of their nation's ability to sustain them. Some nations may even be asked to integrate their forces with those of another, so that a contribution may, for example, consist of an infantry company containing platoons from different countries. **The only constant is that a decision to "join in" is, in every case, a calculated diplomatic decision by each potential member of a coalition or alliance.** The nature of their national decisions, in turn, influences the MNTF's command structure. In a parallel command structure, national forces essentially operate under their own doctrine and procedures within the guidelines determined by the strategic national guidance and are not significantly impacted by multinational influences. Under the integrated and LN command structures, more multinational involvement and interaction occurs. As such, this chapter will primarily focus on issues affecting the latter two structures.

b. **Capabilities.** As shown in Figure III-1, numerous factors influence the military capabilities of nations. The operational-level commander must be aware of the specific constraints and capabilities of the forces of participating nations, and consider these differences when assigning missions and conducting operations. MNTF commanders (similar to JTF commanders) at all levels may be required to spend considerable time consulting and negotiating with diplomats, HN officials, local leaders, and others; their role as diplomats should not be underestimated. MNTF commanders will routinely work directly with political authorities in the region. Even within their own command, political limitations and constraints on the employment of the forces can significantly influence daily operations.

c. **Integration.** The fundamental challenge in multinational operations is the effective integration and synchronization of available assets toward the achievement of common objectives. This goal may be achieved through unity of effort despite disparate (and occasionally incompatible) capabilities, ROE, equipment, and procedures. To reduce disparities among participating forces, minimum capability standards should be established and a certification process developed by the MNFC. Identified shortcomings should be

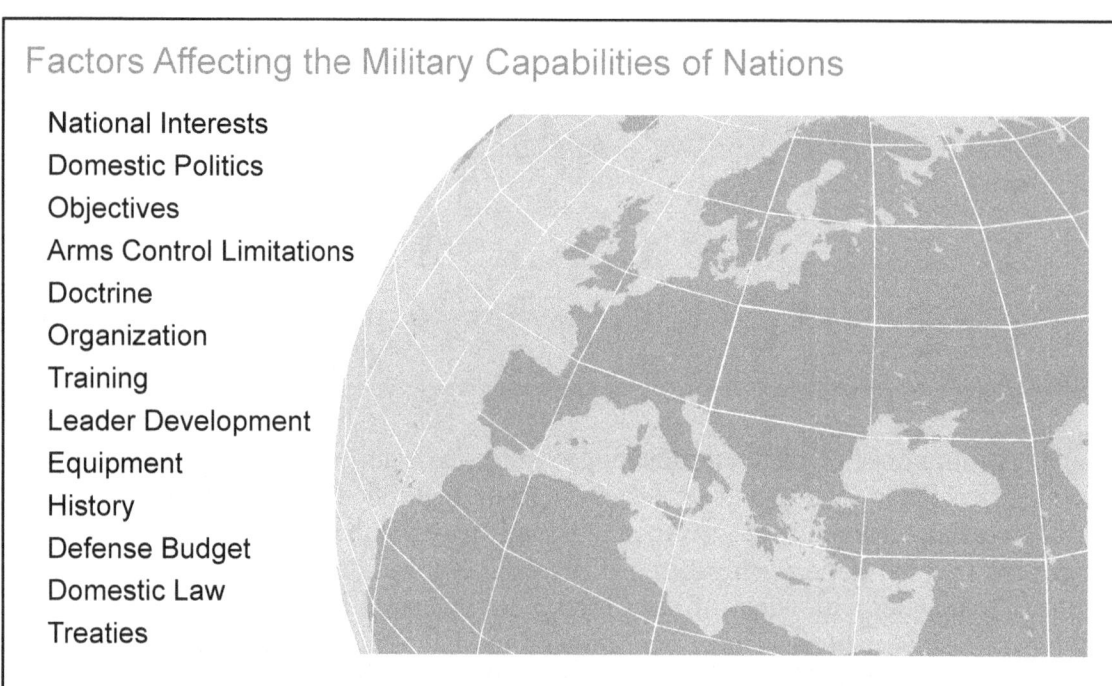

Factors Affecting the Military Capabilities of Nations

National Interests
Domestic Politics
Objectives
Arms Control Limitations
Doctrine
Organization
Training
Leader Development
Equipment
History
Defense Budget
Domestic Law
Treaties

Figure III-1. Factors Affecting the Military Capabilities of Nations

satisfied by either bilateral or multilateral support agreements (formal or informal) prior to the deployment of forces to the OA. This process relies heavily upon detailed coordination between national leadership, prospective forces, and the MNFC. The degree of involvement of each participant is likely to be primarily a political decision and commanders at all levels must be cognizant of national mandates placed on individual units.

d. **Preparation.** In addition to planning and preparing for contingency operations in a multinational environment, CCDRs are responsible to pursue national strategic end states as they develop their theater or functional strategies. This translates into an integrated set of shaping actions and activities by means of an operation or campaign plan.

(1) SC activities are long-term and designed to promote an acceptable state of peace and security in a country or region and preclude or mitigate crises by mobilizing cooperation and building relationships to enhance an HN's or region's security. A multinational operation can be designed to support a CCMD's operation or campaign plan, or a contingency operation.

(2) SC activities are undertaken well in advance of any crisis-precipitating event. The military contribution to these efforts focuses on mobilizing cooperation and building and sustaining relationships to enhance regional security.

(3) A representative listing of SC activities might include:

(a) Provide training, education, and equipment to build the capacity and capability of partner nations and organizations;

(b) Conduct activities with partner nations to confront threats and challenges before they mature into a crisis;

(c) Conduct military-to-military senior leader and staff talks and exchanges;

(d) Promote regional cooperation to meet shared challenges as well as decrease tension and rivalries;

(e) Conduct bilateral and multilateral exercises; and

(f) Conclude formal arrangements for the use of facilities, basing, or transit of military forces.

e. **Employment.** In most multinational operations, the differing degrees of national interest result in varying levels of commitment by partner nations. While some countries might authorize the full range of employment, other countries may limit their forces to strictly defensive or combat service support roles. Some examples of partner nation contributions can be seen in Figure III-2. However, offers of national support should not be declined outright. Instead, every offer should be vetted through the MNFC and multinational partners, and recognized as support to the operation or campaign. This process helps maintain the support of allies, friends, and partners and enhances the relationship. Additionally, multinational support will help increase the perceived legitimacy of operations domestically as well as internationally.

For additional information regarding legitimacy, see JP 3-0, Joint Operations. *For NATO operations, see Allied Joint Publication (AJP)-3,* Allied Joint Doctrine for the Conduct of Operations.

2. Building and Maintaining a Multinational Force

a. Building an MNF starts with the political decisions and diplomatic efforts to create a coalition or spur an alliance into action. Discussion and coordination between potential participants will initially seek to sort out basic questions at the national strategic level. These senior-level discussions could include organizations like the UN or NATO, existing coalitions or alliances, or individual nations. The result of these discussions should determine:

(1) The nature and limits of the response.

(2) The command structure of the response force.

(3) The essential strategic guidance for the response force to include military objectives and the desired end states.

b. **Command Issues.** When the response force is resident within an alliance, the procedures and structure of the alliance will normally determine operational-level leadership for the response force. When the response force is based in a coalition (or an LN structure in an alliance), the designated LN will normally select the operational-level leadership. The

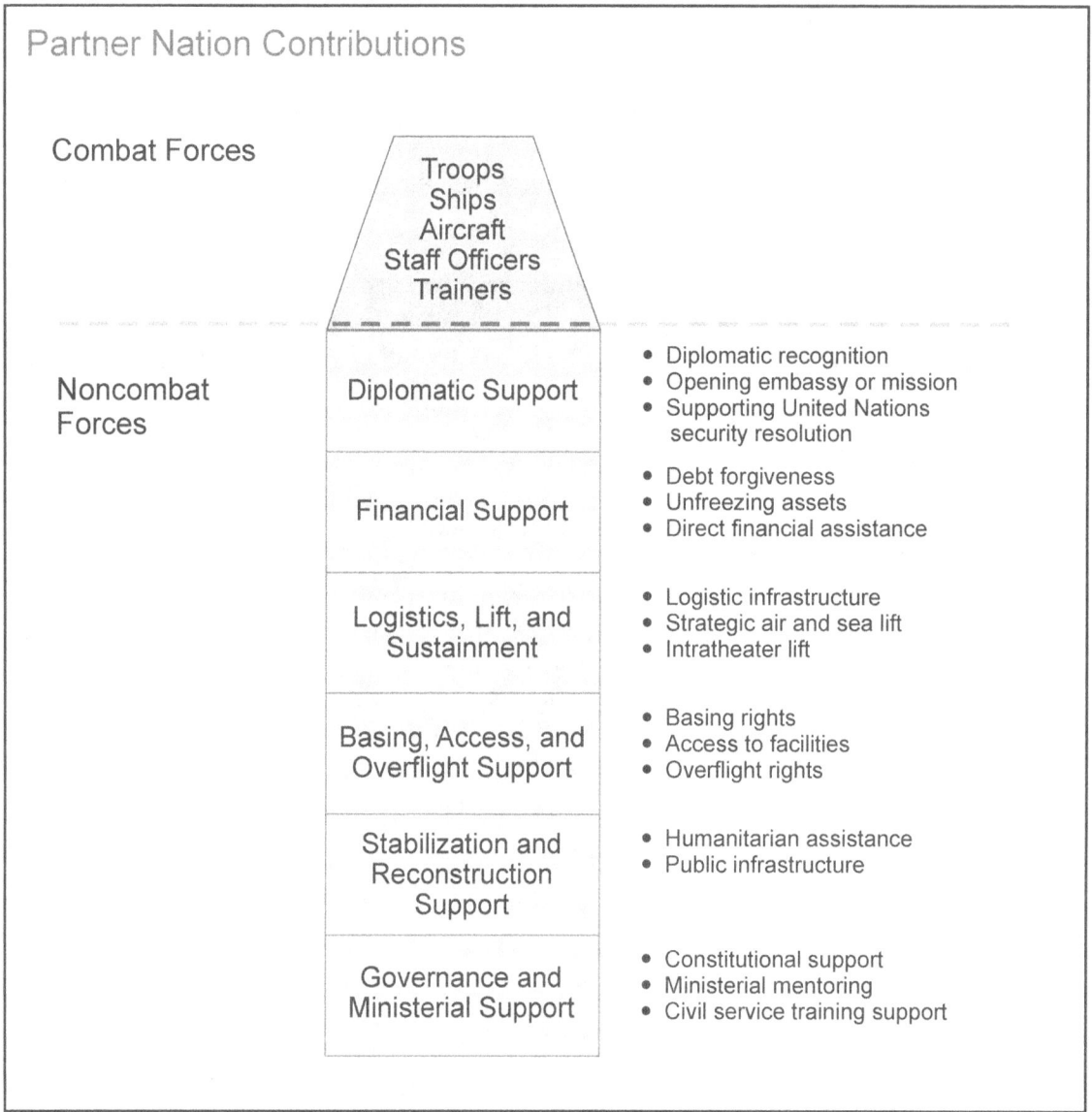

Figure III-2. Partner Nation Contributions

MIC's *Coalition Building Guide,* which describes the LN construct, could be used by an LN and potential partners as a starting point to address the coalition building process as it applies to multinational military operations, particularly at the strategic level.

c. These designated military leaders will coordinate military requirements and actions between participating nations. In an alliance such as NATO, this would normally be the alliance's military commander. The MNFC promulgates essential guidance to all members that should contain the following information:

(1) Purpose of the multinational operation.

(2) Mission statement for the MNTF.

(3) Strategic end state and military end state for the MNTF.

(4) Strategic objectives and broad tasks for the MNTF with guidance for termination or transition.

(5) Participating nations and expected initial contributions.

(6) Designated LN and supporting guidance.

(7) Common security interests.

(8) Multinational communications strategy.

(9) Specific diplomatic, economic, and informational guidance and national limitations, concerns, or sensitivities.

d. When dealing with partner nations, sensitivities and cultural differences must be recognized and acknowledged and procedures developed to mitigate or minimize additional conflict between nations. Some planning considerations for multinational operations may include culture, diet, alcohol consumption policies, male/female cohabitation policies, work hours, leave, and other duty limitations.

e. Maintaining a cohesive MNF may require the MNF commander's continual attention as nearly every action or event may impact national military and political interests and may compete for primacy with the MNF's objective and end state. In some cases, national restrictions may seem wholly out of line with national contributions. This tension between national elements is not new, and commanders at all levels should be prepared to deal with it. As discussed earlier, nations join multinational efforts for a variety of reasons, both known and unknown. National will, popular support, and the perceived achievement of stated objectives are just some of the factors that might influence continued national participation. However, thorough pre-mission preparation and planning can pay significant dividends later as the MNFC faces the challenge of maintaining a stable MNF.

3. Mission Analysis and Assignment of Tasks

a. The MNFC's staff should conduct a detailed mission analysis. This is one of the most important tasks in planning multinational operations and should result in a revised mission statement, commander's intent, and the MNFC's planning guidance. As part of the mission analysis, force requirements should be identified; standards for participation published (e.g., training-level competence and logistics, including deployment, sustainment, and redeployment capabilities); and funding requests, certification procedures, and force commitments solicited from an alliance or likely coalition partners.

b. Before the MNTF staff can develop proposed courses of action (COAs), the MNFC must conduct an estimate of the situation. This will allow the MNFC to analyze, in an organized manner, the many factors that will affect the accomplishment of the assigned mission(s). This estimate should address the respective capabilities, political will, and national interests of the MNTF components. Additionally, expected interagency contributions and involvement of each nation should be addressed. This is a critical step as each nation determines its contribution to the operation. **National force commitments, even**

in an established alliance, are not automatic. For example, a NATO non-Article 5 crisis response operation is one such case where nations can opt in or out based on their national interests. Based upon these national contributions, and after determining the tasks necessary to achieve the objectives that support mission accomplishment, the MNFC should assign specific tasks to the elements of the MNTF most capable of completing those tasks. If there are several different national elements that can complete a particular task, the MNFC should consider assigning that task in a manner that allows each troop contributing nation to make meaningful contributions to the end state.

4. Language, Culture, and Sovereignty

a. **Language. Differing languages within an MNF can present a real challenge to C2, efficient communications, and unity of effort.** US forces cannot assume that the predominant language will automatically be English, and specifying an official language for the MNF can be a sensitive issue. Therefore, US forces should make every effort to overcome language barriers. Wherever and whenever possible, exchange officers or liaison officers (LNOs) or nonmilitary translators should be used to facilitate interaction and coordination with HN forces. Communication is conveyed through both verbal and nonverbal means, with information loss, miscommunications, and misunderstandings having a negative impact on operations. The additional time required to receive information, process it, develop plans from it, translate the plans, and distribute them to multinational partners can adversely impact the speed and tempo of operations. Commanders may lessen these difficulties by early identification of linguist support. They should assess the capabilities of US personnel to communicate with and to understand partners and use properly trained multilingual personnel as appropriate. Capability gaps may be mitigated through the use of contractor support for interpreters and translators and should be addressed during the planning phase. HN resources may serve an especially important role in this capacity, particularly if available during the initial stages of the deployment. In addition, the importance of staffing the HQ with qualified liaison personnel cannot be minimized. This will usually place additional demands upon US commanders for liaison personnel, but they are critical to the success of any multinational mission.

b. **Linguists and Area Experts.** To assist with cultural and language challenges, the MNTF employs linguists and area experts, often available within and through the Service components or from other governmental agencies. In some instances, members of Service forces may be especially familiar with the OA, its cultures, and languages as a result of special training (e.g., foreign area officers), previous assignments, or heritage. The use of such abilities should be maximized to facilitate understanding and communications. Contract linguists should be screened for security purposes and vetted to verify their abilities.

c. **Culture.** Each partner in multinational operations possesses a unique cultural identity—the result of their physical environment, economic, political, and social outlook, as well as the values, beliefs, and symbols that comprise their culture. Even seemingly minor differences, such as dietary restrictions, can have great impact. Commanders should strive to accommodate religious holidays, prayer calls, and other unique cultural traditions important to allies and coalition members, consistent with the situation.

(1) There are a number of tools that can aid commanders and joint forces in identifying and becoming familiar with troop contributing nations' cultural tendencies and provide insights into other cultures (HN, neighboring countries, potential adversaries, and supporters). This may allow commanders to be more effective when interacting with their other MNF leaders and the local populace. These tools can potentially assist commanders in making more timely assessments of potential cultural impacts and minimize any detrimental impact on operations and allow for a more cohesive relationship with our multinational partners and friends.

(2) Some tools that provide analytical methodology for cultural evaluation include:

(a) Joint Knowledge Online Culture and Language at https://www.us.army.mil/suite/designer.

(b) Defense Language Institute/Foreign Language Center at http://www.dliflc.edu/products.html.

(c) US Air Force Language, Region, and Culture Program at http://www.culture.af.mil/.

(d) US Army Training and Doctrine Command Culture Center at https://ikn.army.mil/apps/tccv2.

(e) US Navy Center for Language, Regional Expertise and Culture.

(f) US Marine Corps Intelligence Activity at http://www.quantico.usmc.mil/activities/?Section=MCIA or https://www.intelink.gov/mcia/.

(g) SOF global assessments conducted by United States Special Operations Command.

(h) Marine Corps Center for Advanced Operational Culture Learning https://www.tecom.usmc.mil/caocl/SitePages/Home.aspx.

d. **Sovereignty Issues.** Sovereignty issues will be among the most difficult problems the MNFC may be required to mitigate. Often, the MNFC will be required to accomplish the mission through coordination, communication, and consensus, in addition to traditional command concepts. Political sensitivities must be recognized and acknowledged.

(1) The US commander, as part of the MNF, should coordinate with DOS, country teams, and the ambassador/chief of mission to the respective HN, if available, on any sovereignty issues which cannot be resolved at the MNFC level. Examples of sovereignty issues include basing, civil or criminal jurisdiction over military and contract personnel, immigration, customs, claims, ground movement, overflight rights, aerial ports of debarkation, seaports of debarkation, railheads, border crossings, frequency management, and operations in the territorial sea.

(a) Normally, such issues will be formally resolved with HNs through the development of appropriate technical agreements to augment existing or recently developed status-of-forces agreements (SOFAs) or status of mission agreements. These agreements, negotiated between the HN and the sponsoring organization on behalf of the participating countries, establish the detailed legal status of MNFs.

(b) Authority to negotiate a SOFA is held at the national level. For US forces, some specified portions of that authority have been delegated to the Joint Staff and CCDRs. Neither the MNFC nor the staff has such authority without specific approval or delegation from higher authority. Before any negotiations or agreement with another nation, the SJA or appropriate legal authorities should be consulted. US forces remain subject to the Uniform Code of Military Justice, which will be administered by the appropriate US commander.

(2) The commander may also create structures such as committees to address sovereignty issues. These committees may be chaired by military or nonmilitary representatives of the HN to facilitate cooperation and build trust. These organizations could facilitate operations by reducing sensitivities and misunderstandings and removing impediments. In many cases, SC organizations, NGOs, and IGOs resident in the HN can help establish good will with the HN. In some cases, these organizations may also be called upon to assist in the conduct of operations or in establishing a congenial relationship in the HN.

5. Legal

a. Commanders must ensure that MNTF forces comply with applicable national and international laws during the conduct of all military operations. Participating nations should provide commanders with access to legal advice throughout the operation to facilitate a comprehensive understanding of any national differences. In operations under the authority of NATO, relevant alliance documents will be applicable.

b. US forces will comply with the law of war (also referred to as the law of armed conflict [LOAC]) during all armed conflicts and in all other military operations. Additionally, US forces will be trained in the law of war. US forces will report all possible, suspected, or alleged violations of the law of war (for which there is credible information or conduct during military operations that would constitute a violation of the law of war if it occurred during an armed conflict) through command channels.

Refer to DODD 2311.01E, DOD Law of War Program, *and CJCSI 5810.01D,* Implementation of the DOD Law of War Program.

c. **International Agreements.** The Armed Forces of the United States are committed to conducting joint and multinational operations according to the applicable provisions of the LOAC, including those of The Hague and Geneva Conventions. International agreements are the primary source of rules of international law applicable to US, multinational, and HN forces. The most comprehensive are SOFAs; however, these may be modified or become inapplicable in time of armed conflict. They prescribe most of the reciprocal rights, powers, duties, privileges, and immunities of the US forces to include DOD civilians and contractor personnel stationed abroad and of the governments of the host and partner nations and their respective armed forces. Other important types of international agreements concern security assistance and HN support agreements. For specific information on HN support agreements (e.g., acquisition and cross-servicing agreements [ACSAs]) and international agreements (e.g., defense cooperation agreements), contact the US embassy military senior defense official or GCC's legal advisor.

d. **Treatment of Detainees.** During the conduct of military operations, MNF personnel must be prepared to detain a wide variety of individuals who fall into different categories under the law of war. Regardless of the category or status of a detainee, MNFs are required to properly control, maintain, protect, and account for all detainees IAW applicable domestic law, international law, and policy. Additionally, US forces should be aware that other participating nations may categorize detainees differently. For this reason, and because the excessive use of force or the perceived mistreatment of detainees can also seriously undermine public confidence in MNF operations, it is imperative that commanders provide clear guidance for detainee operations in a multinational environment.

For additional information, see JP 3-63, Detainee Operations.

e. The DOD Detainee Program establishes overarching DOD detainee policy. The directive requires humane treatment of all detainees, however characterized, during all armed conflicts and in all other military operations. The standards of treatment set forth in the directive apply to all DOD components and DOD contractors assigned to or supporting the DOD components engaged in, conducting, participating in, or supporting detainee operations. These standards also apply to all non-DOD personnel as a condition of permitting access to internment facilities or to detainees under DOD control.

For additional information, see DODD 2310.01E, The Department of Defense Detainee Program.

f. **Military Justice**

(1) Jurisdiction over US forces suspected of committing a criminal offense will be decided on a case-by-case basis IAW applicable international agreements with HN civil authorities. It is US policy to retain jurisdiction in all criminal cases to the fullest extent possible. Foreign military commanders exercising operational control (OPCON) or tactical control (TACON) over US forces will not administer discipline.

(2) Jurisdiction over non-US members of the MNTF in such circumstances will also be decided IAW applicable international agreements with HN civil authorities. Since national procedures with regard to jurisdiction will determine how each case will be handled, US commanders should defer such matters to the participating nation's authorities.

g. Commanders should coordinate with the joint force SJA to assist in resolving potential legal conflicts that arise during multinational operations, such as jurisdictional issues related to HN law and military justice, questions regarding compliance with international law, and issues related to the treatment of detainees. However, this does not relieve the commander of the responsibility to understand and apply pertinent directives related to the law of war and ROE.

6. Doctrine and Training

a. **Doctrine.** Some nations possess doctrine and training programs with a full treatment of strategic, operational, and tactical issues. Other nations have doctrine and training programs smaller in both scope and capability to match their national goals and objectives. When the Armed Forces of the United States participate in multinational operations, US commanders should follow multinational doctrine and procedures that have been ratified by the US. For multinational doctrine and procedures not ratified by the US, commanders should evaluate and follow the multinational command's doctrine and procedures where applicable and consistent with US law, policy, and guidance. An example is the MNF SOP developed by 31 nations within the MPAT in the Asia - Pacific region. It seeks to identify common starting points for the rapid activation and forming of an MNTF for crisis response situations (see Appendix B, "Multinational Planning Augmentation Team").

b. **Training and Resources.** When the situation permits, MNFCs at all levels should seek opportunities to improve the contributions of member nation forces through training assistance and resource sharing consistent with agreements between MNF members. This could include the sale or loan of equipment, consistent and shared doctrine, common TTP, and participation in multinational exercises including training at US national training centers when appropriate. GCCs should include this information in their SC part of the TCP.

7. Funding and Resources

Financial and resource considerations may vary greatly with each multinational operation. Responsible parties need to become familiar with the added legal complexities and ramifications when operating with MNFs. Reimbursement and other funding issues are often complex. Many arrangements will be similar to those for UN operations while other financial arrangements will be based on specific coalition agreements, MOUs, or technical agreements. It is important to begin coordination of financial arrangements with prospective multinational partners as early in the planning process as possible. Often, financial arrangements may be supported by special US logistic and funding authorities. Examples of unique authorities include the provision of supplies, services, transportation, and logistic support to coalition forces supporting military and stability operations in Iraq and Afghanistan (Public Law 109-289, Section 9008) and authorities to use ACSAs to lend certain military equipment to foreign forces in Iraq and Afghanistan for personnel protection and survivability (Public Law 109-364, Section 1202).

In addition to the specific agreements governing each operation, important references on multinational funding issues are contained in DOD 7000.14-R, Department of Defense Financial Management Regulation (DODFMR), Security Assistance Policy and Procedures.

8. Protection of Personnel, Information, and Critical Assets

a. The protection function focuses on preserving the joint forces fighting potential in four primary ways. One way uses active defensive measures that protect the joint force, its information, its bases, necessary infrastructure, and lines of communications (LOCs) from an enemy attack. Another way uses passive defensive measures that make friendly forces, systems, and facilities difficult to locate, strike, and destroy. Equally important is the application of technology and procedures to reduce the risk of friendly fire. Finally, emergency management and response reduce the loss of personnel and capabilities due to accidents, health threats, and natural disasters. As the MNFC's mission requires, the protection function also extends beyond force protection to encompass protection of noncombatants; the forces, systems, and civil infrastructure of friendly nations; and interorganizational partners.

See JP 3-0, Joint Operations, *for additional information on the protection function.*

b. Commanders must understand that other nations do not necessarily execute force protection in the same way as the US Armed Forces. Some nations' armed forces may or may not be willing or able to assume the same risk as US forces. US commanders, whether under US control or under a command relationship to a MNF, must continuously assess threats and vulnerabilities while implementing appropriate force protection countermeasures IAW published GCC directives. Special consideration must be given to personnel with duties that require interaction with local populations.

c. Throughout multinational operations, risk management techniques and methodologies should be used to reduce or offset risk by systematically identifying, assessing, and controlling risk.

d. Another significant problem facing the MNF is the potential for friendly fire. Unfamiliar procedures, lack of a common language, and differing operational terms of reference can increase this risk. MNF support or liaison teams can greatly assist in assessing and reducing the friendly fire risk to the MNF by recommending operational coordination measures and technological solutions.

e. Finally, commanders must understand that US forces, as part of a MNF, can potentially be the greater target. Adversaries may view attacks against US Service members as a particularly effective tactic, especially when using co-opted multinational or HN forces to conduct these attacks against unsuspecting US forces. While these types of so-called "insider" or "green on blue" attacks may be context-specific to a particular theater, JFCs should nevertheless ensure that their protection plans at least take into account the potential for these types of attacks and plan appropriate countermeasures as the situation dictates. **US forces operating at tactical levels may be especially vulnerable to unintended and adverse exploitative use of information to gain advantage. Commanders should implement clear measures to ensure tactical information is accurate, timely, and adequately protected at all times.**

f. Nontraditional threats, such as insider attacks, undermine an MNF's ability in establishing a secure and stable environment as well as the cohesion of the MNFs. Strategically, these types of threats provide a propaganda platform from which adversaries can not only threaten the MNF's objectives, goals, and exit strategy but also undermine the overall efforts of the international community. Tactically, the breakdown of trust, communication, and cooperation between HN and MNFs affects military capability. Eliminating or minimizing nontraditional threats, especially by proper preparation and training of coalition forces, is critical to mission success. However, tougher force protection standards and measures that are overtly heavy handed must be well balanced yet culturally sensitive enough to not send the wrong message to the very people and organizations the coalition is trying to protect.

g. Commanders must recognize that force protection may have a higher priority than attainment of specific tactical objectives as the information gained by an adversary's successful attack against US forces can have an operational or even strategic impact. This does not imply that what is called for is a reduction of risk by isolation of US forces. Proactive engagement has historically constituted a more effective tactic than mere risk avoidance.

9. Rules of Engagement

a. Obtaining concurrence for ROE from national authorities may be time-consuming but is essential and should begin early in the planning process. Even though the participants may have similar political mandates, ROE may differ among the nations represented. In many cases, commanders of deployed member forces may lack the authority to speak on behalf of their nation in the ROE development process. Complete consensus or standardization of ROE should be sought but may not be achievable. In any event, the MNFC should reconcile differences as much as possible to develop and implement simple ROE that can be tailored by member forces to their national policies and law.

b. It is essential that adjacent or mutually supporting formations and forces understand each others' ROE, as it cannot be assumed that each will react in an identical fashion to a given situation. Without this understanding, events could result in misperceptions, confusion, and even friendly fire.

c. US forces assigned OPCON or TACON to an MNFC will follow the ROE of the MNF for mission accomplishment, if authorized by SecDef. US forces retain the right of self-defense. Apparent inconsistencies between the right of self-defense contained in US ROE and the MNF ROE will be submitted through the US chain of command for resolution. While the final resolution is pending, US forces will continue to operate under US ROE. In the case of NATO operations, attention should be directed to applicable alliance documents, such as, Military Committee 362/1, *NATO Rules of Engagement.*

For additional information on standing rules of engagement, see CJCSI 3121.01B, Standing Rules of Engagement/Standing Rules for the Use of Force for US Forces.

10. Combat Identification and Friendly Fire Prevention

Tragically, "fog-of-war" situations can lead to friendly fire incidents. A key survivability enabler, to mitigate friendly fire incidents, is the rapid, reliable identification of friends, foes, and neutrals, also known as combat identification (CID).

a. Effective CID enhances joint force capabilities by providing confidence in the accuracy of engagement decisions throughout the force. The MNFC's CID procedures should serve to optimize mission effectiveness by maximizing enemy engagements while minimizing friendly fire and collateral damage. These measures particularly are important in PO and traditional noncombat operations. Therefore, CID measures should be established early in the planning cycle.

b. CID considerations play an important role in force protection. The MNFC's CID procedures must be consistent with ROE and not interfere with a unit's or an individual's ability to engage enemy forces and conduct actions appropriate for self-defense. CID characterizations, when applied with ROE, enable engagement decisions and the subsequent use, or prohibition of use, of lethal weapons and nonlethal capabilities. When developing the MNF CID procedures, important considerations include the missions, capabilities, and limitations of all participants.

For additional guidance on CID, refer to JP 3-09, Joint Fire Support.

c. MNFCs must make every effort to reduce the potential for the unintentional killing or wounding of friendly personnel (to include civilians) by friendly fire. The destructive power and range of modern weapons, coupled with the high intensity and rapid tempo of modern combat, the fluid nature of the nonlinear OA, the changing disposition of attacking and defending forces, and the presence of civilians in the OA increase the potential for friendly fire.

d. Commanders must identify and assess situations that increase the risk of friendly fire in the OE and institute appropriate preventive measures. The primary preventive measures for limiting and reducing friendly fire are command emphasis, disciplined operations, close coordination among component commands and multinational partners, exercises, reliable and timely CID, effective SOPs, technology solutions (e.g., identify friend or foe, friendly force tracking), and enhanced situational awareness (SA) of the OE. Commanders should seek to minimize friendly fire while not limiting boldness and initiative.

SECTION B. OPERATIONAL CONSIDERATIONS

11. Intelligence

a. In most multinational operations, the JFC will be required to share intelligence with foreign military forces and to coordinate receiving intelligence from those forces. In some circumstances, the JFC will need to seek authority to go outside the usual political-military channels to provide information to NGOs. Unique intelligence policy and dissemination criteria will have to be tailored to each multinational operation.

b. A multinational intelligence center is necessary for merging and prioritizing the intelligence requirements from each participating nation and for acquiring and fusing all the nations' intelligence contributions. Likewise, the center should coordinate the intelligence collection planning and intelligence, surveillance, and reconnaissance operations of each nation. The multinational intelligence center should include representatives from all nations participating in the multinational operation. Designating a single director of intelligence for the multinational command may assist in resolving potential disagreements among the multinational members.

c. Every interrelated intelligence operation of the intelligence process—planning and direction, collection, processing and exploitation, analysis and production, dissemination and integration, and evaluation and feedback—is substantively affected in multinational operations. In some international operations or campaigns, JFCs will be able to use ISAs (e.g., NATO STANAG) as a basis for establishing rules and policies for conducting joint intelligence operations. Since each multinational operation will be unique, such agreements may have to be modified or amended based on the situation. The following general principles provide a starting point for creating the necessary policy and procedures (see Figure III-3).

(1) **Maintain Unity of Effort.** Each nation's intelligence personnel need to view the threat from multinational as well as national perspectives. A threat to one element of an MNF by the common adversary must be considered a threat to all MNF elements.

(2) **Make Adjustments.** There will be differences in intelligence doctrine and procedures among the coalition partners. A key to effective multinational intelligence is the willingness to make the adjustments required to resolve significant differences such as:

(a) How intelligence is provided to the commander, the commander's staff, and forces.

(b) Procedures for sharing information among intelligence agencies.

(c) The degree of security afforded by different communications systems and procedures.

(d) Administrative requirements.

(3) **Plan Early and Plan Concurrently.** National command channels determine what intelligence may be shared with the forces of other nations early in the planning process. NATO and the US, as well as the US and the Republic of Korea, via the Combined

---

Multinational Intelligence Principles

- Maintain unity of effort.
- Make adjustments.
- Plan early and plan concurrently.
- Share all necessary information.
- Conduct complementary operations.

Figure III-3. Multinational Intelligence Principles

Forces Command, have developed and exercised intelligence policies and procedures that provide examples of how multinational planning can be done in advance.

(4) **Share All Necessary Information**

(a) Coalition members should share all relevant and pertinent intelligence about the situation and adversary consistent with national disclosure policy (NDP) and theater guidance. However, information about intelligence sources and methods should not be shared with coalition members unless approved by the appropriate authority.

(b) Force protection is a mission inherent to any commander, and intelligence support to that mission is critical. Every effort must be made to share any data that could impact the commander's force protection mission.

(c) When information relating to a particular source cannot be shared, the intelligence derived from that source should still be provided to other multinational partners if at all possible. The intelligence directorate of a joint staff (J-2) should establish procedures for separating intelligence from sources and methods. Intelligence agencies often produce highly classified reports that contain compartmented information. To the greatest extent possible, this information should be disseminated using a tear line. A tear line enables the J-2 and Service component intelligence elements to keep information above the tear line (compartmented data) and disseminate the intelligence below. Having intelligence production agencies use such tear lines should facilitate intelligence sharing. Such considerations warrant increased emphasis for forces operating at the tactical level where timely information is especially critical to mission success as well as prevention of friendly fire and undesired collateral damage. When feasible, intelligence production organizations operating in a multinational environment should implement a write for release without dissemination restrictions policy to facilitate timely dissemination of tactical intelligence partner organizations.

(d) The joint force J-2 should obtain the necessary authorizations from the foreign disclosure officers (FDOs) and designated intelligence disclosure officials (DIDOs) from the CCMD J-2 or FDO as soon as possible. J-2 personnel should be knowledgeable of the specific foreign disclosure policy, procedures, and regulations for the operation. The assignment and use of qualified and certified FDOs and DIDOs are vital to safeguarding classified information from inadvertent disclosure and will enhance the efficient flow of intelligence.

(5) **Conduct Complementary Operations**

(a) Intelligence efforts of the nations should be complementary. Each nation will have intelligence system strengths and limitations and unique and valuable capabilities. HN security services' capabilities, for example, may contribute significantly to force protection. Furthermore, planning with friendly nations to fill shortfalls, especially linguist requirements, may help overcome such limitations.

(b) All intelligence resources and capabilities should be made available for application to the whole of the intelligence problem. Establishing a multinational collection

UNITED STATES CENTRAL COMMAND
COALITION INTELLIGENCE CENTER

"We were established in 2001 at the beginning of Operation ENDURING FREEDOM. Under J-2 [intelligence directorate of a joint staff] we were established for the purpose of facilitating and sharing of intelligence. In the beginning there was some operational tactical intelligence that we shared with our coalition members and that information was limited to just Afghanistan. But as the mission expanded into Iraq, we also had to expand our purpose of sharing and discussing information while establishing analytical teams to address specific questions from both the Coalition and the US. Our Center is the forum where most of those discussions take place.

The Coalition countries are all invited to have membership in the Intelligence Center. We put in perspective the nation's involvement with operations. Not every country has an intelligence interest and not every country has an intelligence officer assigned to US Central Command (USCENTCOM). Those that do have an intelligence officer assigned at USCENTCOM will participate with us on a daily basis. Those that do not have an intelligence officer, but do have intelligence interests, usually go through their country's senior national representative or through the operations officer to consult with us and discuss with us issues of common interest."

Colonel Evilio Otero, Jr.
Chief, Coalition Intelligence Center
USCENTCOM Coalition Village

management element is essential for planning and coordinating multinational collection operations.

See JP 2-0, Joint Intelligence, for further details. Additional guidance on intelligence operations in multinational operations can be found in JP 2-01, Joint and National Intelligence Support to Military Operations.

d. **Geospatial Intelligence Geodetic Datums.** Multinational operations require interoperable geodetic data, applications, and data exchange capabilities. Whenever possible, participants should agree to work on standard vertical and horizontal datums that allow products to have common datum reference points. A multinational geodetic reference plan should be developed and used to coordinate all products for use by member forces, including access approval procedures and blending assets into a cohesive production program.

See JP 2-03, Geospatial Intelligence Support to Joint Operations, for further details.

e. **Biometrics.** Biometrics is the process of recognizing an individual based on measurable anatomical, physiological, and behavioral characteristics. MNFs are employing biometrics in operations with increasing frequency and improving results to identify known threats, disrupt adversary freedom of movement within the populace, link people to events, and verify local and third-country nationals accessing MNF bases and facilities. The ability

"Coalition forces continue to play a vital role in current, and likely all future operations in the US Central Command (USCENTCOM) area of responsibility (AOR). The information sharing challenge is extremely complicated with multiple coalitions, international organizations, and alliances participating in different operations. Many nations participate in multiple communities. These include the 66-nation Global Counterterrorism Forces, the 51-nation Multinational Coalition Forces-Iraq, the 11-nation Combined Naval Forces Central Command, the 33-nation International Security Assistance Forces for Afghanistan, the 26-member nation North Atlantic Treaty Organization, as well as the traditional 6 Gulf Cooperation Council member states and our 25 regional AOR countries. USCENTCOM needs to be able to electronically share information with these various communities of interests quickly and efficiently to successfully conduct coalition operations."

Jill L. Boardman/Donald W. Shuey
Combined Enterprise Network Theater Information System;
Supporting Coalition Warfare World-Wide
April 2004

to accurately identify or verify an individual is a critical component of force protection. Biometrics is an enabling technology which crosscuts many intelligence-related mission sets and functions.

f. **Other Considerations.** It is important to consider the ramifications of labeling information about an OA as intelligence, especially when interacting with nonmilitary organizations. In many cultures, the perception of intelligence connotes information gathered on a nation's citizenry to exploit it. Further, attempts to exchange information with many NGOs would likely be stifled as they strive to maintain political neutrality throughout the world and would not associate in any perceived intelligence gathering attempts. Therefore, unclassified facts and/or data should be referred to as information in order to facilitate its dissemination among members of the MNF for the purpose of fostering mutual interests in resolving or deterring conflict or providing support.

12. Information Sharing

a. **National Disclosure Policy.** The release of classified information to multinational partners is governed by NDP. Detailed guidance must be provided to the senior US commander by the chain of command IAW National Security Decision Memorandum 119, *Disclosure of Classified United States Military Information to Foreign Governments and International Organizations,* and NDP-1, *National Policy and Procedures for the Disclosure of Classified Military Information to Foreign Governments and International Organizations.* Detailed written guidance may be supplemented with limited delegation of disclosure authority where appropriate (e.g., combined force protection purposes). However, the senior US officer needs to become personally concerned with the issues of intelligence sharing and releasing of information early in the process and clearly state the commander's requirements. Commanders should promote information sharing and inclusion of LNOs in secured systems as much as possible. Commanders should establish and promulgate clear NDP-compliant guidance to subordinate elements that permit flexibility to share information where and when it is needed.

b. The NDP is implemented within DOD by DODD 5230.11, *Disclosure of Classified Military Information to Foreign Governments and International Organizations,* and CJCSI 5221.01, *Delegation of Authority to Commanders of Combatant Commands to Disclose Classified Military Information to Foreign Governments and International Organizations.*

JP 2-01, Joint and National Intelligence Support to Military Operations, *contains a detailed discussion of sanitization and foreign disclosure procedures.*

c. Military information and intelligence should be derived and crafted to maximize recipient eligibility. Such principles as accessible, timely electronic dissemination and scalable classification levels (e.g., tear lines) are just a few of the multiple techniques to enhance sharing. Intelligence and information should be written for release at the lowest possible classification level and given the fewest possible dissemination restrictions within foreign disclosure guidelines. This is important in maintaining the integrity of a common holistic understanding of the OE. Other nations are also likely to have access to their own national intelligence and should be encouraged to share across MNFs.

d. Although there may be no clearly defined threat, the essential elements of US military operations should be safeguarded. The uncertain nature of the situation, coupled with the potential for rapid change, requires that operations security (OPSEC) be an integral part of any operation. OPSEC planners must consider the effect of media coverage and the possibility that coverage may compromise essential security or disclose critical information.

See DODD 5205.02, DOD Operations Security (OPSEC) Program, *for more information.*

e. The success of joint and multinational operations and interagency coordination hinges upon timely and accurate information and intelligence sharing. Information sharing, cooperation, collaboration, and coordination are enabled by an intelligence and information sharing environment that fully integrates joint, multinational, and interagency partners in a collaborative enterprise. The JFC participating in the coalition or alliance tailors the policy and procedures for that particular operation based on national and theater guidance. In some multinational operations or campaigns, JFCs will be able to use existing ISAs (e.g., NATO) as a basis for establishing rules and policies for conducting joint intelligence operations. Since each multinational operation will be unique, such agreements may have to be modified or amended based on the situation. A JFC participating in a coalition or alliance should tailor the policy and procedures for that particular operation based on theater guidance and national policy as contained in NDP 1, *National Policy and Procedures for the Disclosure of Classified Military Information to Foreign Governments and International Organizations.* NDP 1 provides policy and procedures in the form of specific disclosure criteria and limitations, definition of terms, release arrangements, and other guidance.

f. Information sharing, including intelligence information, plays a critical role in the success of any multinational endeavor. Analysis of recent operational lessons learned emphasizes that multinational operations are much more effective, efficient, and safe when information is shared by all the forces involved. The ability to exchange tactical information is especially critical for forces during execution. Information must flow quickly from sensors to fusion processes to analysts and decision makers, and ultimately to those who execute actions. Some specific insights and recommendations from these operational lessons learned include:

(1) Develop categories/groups in which information can be released or disclosed. Release is the physical transfer to another nation. With disclosure, the owning or originating nation maintains control, but the information may be visually or orally displayed to another nation.

(2) Address information disclosure restrictions before major planning efforts and especially before execution.

(3) Identify, delegate, and announce release authority early and to all concerned.

(4) Identify and pre-stage classified documents (e.g., Adaptive Planning and Execution System plans and orders) to be made releasable and distributed to multinational partners at the right time.

g. **Communications and Processing Architectures.** Due to the perishable nature of pertinent, releasable intelligence, it is imperative that a system be devised for and by the MNF members that is capable of transmitting the most important intelligence rapidly to units. Frequently this system relies on the distribution of standardized equipment by one country's forces to ensure commonality. The system must also be firmly rooted in a network of coalition LNOs at major intelligence production or communication centers, to provide redundant intelligence communications channels to their parent nation, and to determine and obtain intelligence uniquely suited for that nation's mission in time to exploit it.

(1) Several nations maintain separate classified Internet and communications systems. For US forces, the SECRET Internet Protocol Router Network (SIPRNET) is the primary classified architecture.

(2) Unclassified networks are an operational imperative. In addition to classified networks, an unclassified network using the Internet (commercially encrypted if available) is a communications backbone for multinational operations. To allow for timely and efficient information sharing with nonmilitary organizations, the MNF should provide these organizations with access to current information on unclassified networks. MNFs should be aware that many NGOs/IGOs are hesitant to use DOD-sponsored information exchange Web sites in order to avoid the appearance of close association with USG entities. In such situations, MNFs should first coordinate regarding these concerns and then be prepared to "push" information to specified organizational Web sites.

(3) MNF networks should be established to provide responsive information sharing between the MNFs, but care must be taken to avoid the inadvertent sharing of classified information that has not been sanitized for release to other nations. Ideally this mission partner network would provide an operating environment in which partners could plan, prepare, and execute operations at an appropriate, single security classification level, with a

common language. The use of cross network information security solutions should be used whenever possible to avoid the inadvertent sharing of information with networks external to those accessible by the collective membership of a specific MNF. Often, LNOs can bridge the culture gap between what multinational commanders/staffs say and what they mean.

h. **Coordination.** Within alliances, it is common for intelligence procedures, practices, and standardized agreements to be established and tested prior to actual use. Coalitions, however, are frequently created and disbanded relatively quickly. Coalition participants typically compensate for the lack of standardization through coordination between national leadership and prospective forces. As mentioned above, coordinating the elements of communications architectures is essential. Additional areas requiring extensive coordination include the friendly use of the electromagnetic spectrum, use of space and/or space assets, geographical location of intelligence collection assets, and targets of intelligence collection. Intelligence processing centers should be multinational in character, serving the MNFC but also recognizing intelligence that has value in support of national missions. However, establishment of these multinational processing centers, particularly in the case of ad hoc coalitions, will require extensive personal involvement and support from the MNFC and the corresponding nation to make this a functioning reality. The MNFC priority intelligence requirements should serve as the milestones to fully focus the intelligence effort. The answers can only be gained through effective coordination at all levels.

i. Additional national and DOD-level references on information sharing useful to enhancing the information environment in support of joint and/or multinational operations include the *National Strategy for Information Sharing, United States Intelligence Community Information Sharing Strategy, DOD Information Sharing Strategy, and DOD Information Sharing Implementation Plan.* Additionally, the Defense Information Systems Agency has a Multinational Information Sharing Program Office with a mission to manage current multinational information sharing efforts, provide the standard multinational information sharing services and applications for future DOD information networks, and facilitate information sharing among DOD components and eligible foreign nations in support of planning and execution of military operations.

13. **Communications**

a. Communications are fundamental to successful multinational operations. Planning considerations include frequency management, equipment compatibility, procedural compatibility, cryptographic and information security, identification friend or foe, and data-link protocols. MNFCs should anticipate that some forces from MNF will have direct and near immediate communications capability from the OA to their respective national political leadership. This capability can facilitate coordination of issues, but it can also be a source of frustration as leaders external to the OA may be issuing guidance directly to their deployed national forces. Many communications issues can be resolved through equipment exchange and liaison teams. When exchanging equipment, special consideration must be paid to the release of communications security (COMSEC) devices as well as the level and nature of classified information (material) released to individual countries per NDP and any applicable exceptions. The ability of the MNF to exchange information at all levels (i.e., strategic, operational, and tactical) should be a consideration during planning and throughout execution.

b. Communications requirements vary with the mission, size, composition, geography, and location of the MNF. It is critical that operations and communications planners begin the coordination process early to ensure both US and MNF communication requirements are identified and sourced prior to operations. Interoperability is often constrained by the least technologically proficient participant. Effective communications support enables control over diverse, widely dispersed air, maritime, ground, and space elements. Access to both military and commercial satellites should be an early planning requirement to support widely dispersed elements. The MNFC should address the need for integrated communications among all participating forces early in the planning phase of the operation. MNF planning and technical communications systems control centers should be established as soon as possible to coordinate all communications.

For more information regarding frequency management, refer to JP 6-01, Joint Electromagnetic Spectrum Management Operations.

c. In all multinational operations a broadband, unclassified network will be a critical requirement for multinational coordination with all actors within the MNF OA. The IHC and affected nations' governments and militaries will normally use unclassified, commercially encrypted networks as their primary collaboration and coordination tool. US forces should be able to integrate with MNFs to support collaboration needed to conduct multinational operations. US forces should expect to use SIPRNET solely for US-specific communication and tasks not suitable for execution in a multination information sharing environment. Satellite access to broadband Internet capability must be planned as an operational necessity, if not currently available within the MNF OA.

d. LNO teams should be sent to other MNF HQ to facilitate integration of operations. These LNO teams should deploy with sufficient communications equipment to conduct operations with their respective HQ. Consideration should also be given to possible degradation of communications due to the extended distances over which the MNF may operate and the impact of enemy exploitation of the electromagnetic spectrum. Urban operations present other difficulties due to interference from physical structures or frequency overlaps. Planning for communications support also includes provisions which allow execution of required communications under adverse conditions. Additionally, US law requires prior international and implementing agreements defining quid pro quo payments for allied use of the Defense Information Systems Network and military satellite communications assets.

e. Secure C2 systems are vital to the execution of MNF operations to avoid conflict and increase mutual understanding. The goal of secure C2 interoperability within an MNF is to develop greater cooperation through improved technical capability, system interdependence, and SA in the OA.

f. Communications Security Release to Foreign Nations Policy. Disclosing, releasing and transferring products or associated COMSEC information to foreign governments is governed by Department of Defense Instruction (DODI) 8523.01, "Communications Security (COMSEC)." Detailed guidance outlining criteria for release of information security products, services, and information to foreign governments is provided in CJCSI 6510.06, *Communication Security Releases to Foreign Nations*.

g. Under CJCSI 6510.06, *Communications Security Releases to Foreign Nations,* the Chairman of the Joint Chiefs of Staff (CJCS) validates CCMD interoperability requirements to release COMSEC products or associated COMSEC information to any foreign government. These secure C2 interoperability requirements originate from the theater Service components.

h. Release of COMSEC to foreign governments is permitted when there is a validated interoperability requirement. Specifically, the GCC and the MNFC should have or develop agreements on cryptographic, communications and/or automated data processing (ADP) security issues among all multinational components and understand where "capability gaps" exist, along with the implication of those gaps.

14. Operational Environment

a. **Land Operations.** In most multinational operations, land forces are an integral, and central, part of the military effort. The level and extent of land operations in a multinational environment is largely a function of the overall military objectives, any national caveats to employment, and the forces available within the MNF.

(1) National doctrine and training will normally dictate employment options within the MNF. Nations with common TTP will also experience far greater interoperability. Effective use of SC activities may significantly reduce interoperability problems even for countries with widely disparate weapons systems.

(2) The MNFC may assign the responsibility for land operations to an overall multinational force land component commander (MNFLCC) or a task force (TF) within the MNF command structure (for example: TF South, TF North). Such TFs may include elements from a single nation or multiple nations depending on the situation and the interoperability factors of the nations involved. In addition, the MNFC may also assign an area of operations (AO) to the MNFLCC or TF based upon concept of the operations. Figure III-4 contains a representative sample of MNFLCC responsibilities.

(3) The MNFC will also establish supported and supporting relationships between the land component command or TF and other MNTF components (maritime, air, and special operations) based upon mission requirements to assist in prioritizing actions, assist in establishing the main effort, and to establish formal command/coordination channels between the components for a specific operation, mission, or phase.

(4) A fundamental consideration for planning and executing land operations is sustainability. The following factors impact the sustainability of land operations:

Multinational Force Land Component Commander Notional Responsibilities

- Advise the multinational force commander (MNFC) on the proper employment of forces made available for tasking.

- Develop the joint land operation plan/operation order in support of the MNFC's concept of operations and optimizing the operations of task-organized land forces. The multinational force land component commander (MNFLCC) issues planning guidance to all subordinate and supporting elements and analyzes proposed courses of action. The intent is to concentrate combat power at critical times and places to accomplish strategic, operational, and tactical goals.

- Direct the execution of land operations as specified by the MNFC, which includes making timely adjustments to the tasking of forces and capabilities made available. The MNFLCC coordinates changes with affected component commanders as appropriate.

- Coordinate the planning and execution of joint land operations with the other components and supporting agencies.

- Evaluate the results of land operations to include the effectiveness of interdiction operations and forwarding these results to the MNFC to support the combat assessment effort.

- Synchronize and integrate movement and maneuver, fires, and interdiction in support of land operations.

- Designate the target priorities, effects, and timing for joint land operations.

- Establish a personnel recovery (PR) coordination cell (PRCC) to coordinate all component PR activities, including coordination with the joint personnel recovery center (JPRC) and other component PRCCs. Be prepared to establish a JPRC if directed or if designated as the joint force supported commander for PR.

- Provide mutual support to other components by conducting operations such as suppression of enemy air defenses and suppression of threats to maritime operations.

- Coordinate with other nations' functional and Service components in support of accomplishment of MNFC objectives.

- Provide an assistant or deputy to the area air defense commander for land-based joint theater air and missile defense operations and coordination as determined by the MNFC.

- Support the MNFC's information operations (IO) by developing the IO requirements that support land operations and synchronizing the land force IO assets when directed, to include cyberspace requirements.

- Establish standing operating procedures and other directives based on MNFC guidance.

- Provide inputs into the MNFC-approved joint operational area air defense plan and the airspace control plan.

- Integrate the MNFLCC's communications systems and resources into the theater's networked communications system architecture or common operational picture to synchronize MNFLCC's critical voice and data requirements. These communications systems requirements, coordination issues, and capabilities should be considered in the joint planning and execution process.

Figure III-4. Multinational Force Land Component Commander Notional Responsibilities

(a) Personnel staffing requirements.

(b) Medical requirements and capabilities.

(c) Maintenance.

(d) Supply.

(e) Storage facilities.

(f) Transportation.

(g) Technical support and requirements.

(h) Common sourcing of support.

See JP 3-31, Command and Control for Joint Land Operations, *for more detail. See also JP 4-08,* Logistic Support of Multinational Operations. *AJP-3.2,* Allied Joint Doctrine for Land Operations, *provides further information on doctrine for planning, preparing, and executing NATO land component operations.*

b. **Maritime Operations.** In a multinational environment, an operational aim for maritime forces is to exercise sea control or project power ashore, synchronize maritime operations with the other major MNF operational functions of land forces, air forces, and SOF; and support the MNFC's intent and guidance in achieving the MNF mission. Maritime forces are primarily navies; however, they may include maritime-focused air forces, amphibious forces, or other government departments and agencies charged with sovereignty, security, or constabulary functions at sea.

(1) Maritime operational responsibility may be assigned to a multinational force maritime component commander (MNFMCC) or a designated TF. Figure III-5 contains a representative sample of MNFMCC responsibilities.

(2) The MNFC can also assign a maritime AO to the MNFMCC or naval TF within the MNF OA, based upon the concept of operations (CONOPS). The MNFC will also establish supported and supporting relationships between the MNFMCC (or TF) and other MNF components (land, air, special operations forces) based upon mission requirements to assist in prioritizing actions, assist in establishing the main effort, and establish formal command/coordination channels between the components for a specific operation/mission or phase.

(3) A fundamental consideration of maritime operations is sustainability. The following factors impact the sustainability of maritime operations:

(a) Available surface ships (combatant and noncombatant).

(b) Available submarine assets.

Multinational Force Maritime Component Commander Notional Responsibilities

- Recommend to the multinational force commander (MNFC) the apportionment of the joint maritime effort (after consultation with other component commanders).

- Provide maritime forces to other component commanders in accordance with MNFC apportionment decisions.

- Control the execution of joint maritime operations, as specified by the MNFC, to include adjusting targets and tasks for available joint capabilities/forces. The MNFC and affected component commanders will be notified, as appropriate, if the multinational force maritime component commander changes the planned joint maritime operations during execution.

- Assign and coordinate target priorities within the maritime area of operations (AO) and integrate maneuver and movement, fires, and interdiction. The multinational force maritime component commander nominates targets located within the maritime AO to the joint targeting process that may potentially require action by another component commander's assigned forces.

- Contribute to maritime domain awareness. In order to allow decision makers to understand complex security environments, maritime components must:

  ○ Persistently monitor the maritime domain to identify potential and actual maritime threats;

  ○ Fuse and analyze intelligence and information when possible; and

  ○ Disseminate intelligence and information in near real-time to the MNFC and other component commanders.

- Function as the supported/supporting commander, as directed by the MNFC.

- Provide centralized direction for the allocation and tasking of forces/capabilities made available.

- Establish a personnel recovery coordination center in the same manner as the land component commander.

Figure III-5. Multinational Force Maritime Component Commander Notional Responsibilities

(c) Maintenance.

(d) Supply (to include combat logistics force ships).

(e) Storage facilities.

(f) Weather and sea state conditions.

(g) Sea LOCs.

(4) Properly planned, resourced, and employed maritime forces may conduct operations that provide the MNFC with a multifunctional force that can use the maneuver space of the sea to provide a broad range of options, generally unfettered by the requirement to obtain HN permissions and access. Maritime forces can provide power projection, afloat HQ, logistics, area surveillance, and denial platforms and facilities for joint forces offering

---

advantages in flexibility and sustainability. Use of maritime forces may reduce the MNF footprint ashore and allow support and sustainment to be landed in sufficient quantities, as required, without necessarily placing it all in a vulnerable and essentially immobile location. Seabasing of MNFs also reduces the possible negative impact on limited infrastructure ashore and facilitates the protection of supplies and logistics support. Maritime forces expand access options, reduce dependence on land bases, and create uncertainty for adversaries.

(5) Maritime transport vessels provide the bulk of heavy lift in support of multinational operations.

c. **Air Operations**

(1) Air operations provide the MNFC with a responsive and flexible means of operational reach. The MNFC can execute deep operations rapidly, striking at decisive points and attacking centers of gravity. Further, transportation and support requirements can be greatly extended in response to emerging crisis and operational needs. Multinational air operations are focused on supporting the MNFC's intent and guidance in accomplishing the MNTF mission and at the same time, ensuring air operations are integrated with the other major MNF operational functions (land, maritime, and special operations forces).

(2) Overall MNF air operations will normally be assigned to a multinational force air component commander (MNFACC) (the designation will be based on the type of multinational configuration used in the operation). MNFACC responsibilities include the planning, coordinating, allocating, and tasking of air capabilities/force made available based on the MNFC's air apportionment decision (see Figure III-6). The MNFC will also establish supported and supporting relationships between the MNFACC or TF and other MNF components based on MNF mission requirements, to assist in prioritizing actions and to establish formal command/coordination channels between the components for a specific operation/mission or phase.

(3) **Air Operations Planning.** An integral part of the MNFC's planning efforts is the concept of air operations. The MNFACC is responsible for air operations planning, and develops the concept for air operations describing how the multinational assets made available are envisioned to be employed in support of the MNFC's overall objectives. Both US component commanders and MNFCs should provide highly trained liaison staffs to facilitate integration, coordination, and synchronization of their operations. Air planning should also include the use of logistic air assets and airfields. This is especially important for the coordination of tactical air operations with logistic operations, especially the air movement of supplies, their unloading, and rapid clearance from aerial ports. In the event that no established multinational guidance is available, planning considerations for multinational air operations should resemble those for joint air operations.

See JP 3-30, Command and Control for Joint Air Operations, *for details on the air planning process.*

Multinational Force Air Component Commander
Notional Responsibilities

- Develop a multinational air operations plan to support the multinational force commander's (MNFC's) objectives.

- Recommend to the MNFC apportionment of the joint air effort, after consulting with other component commanders.

- Allocate and task air capabilities/forces made available based on the MNFC's air apportionment decision.

- Provide oversight and guidance during execution of multinational air operations.

- Coordinate multinational air operations with other component commanders and forces assigned to or supporting the MNFC.

- Assess the results of multinational air operations.

- Support MNFC information operations with assigned assets, when directed.

- Function as the supported/supporting commander, as directed by the MNFC.

- Perform the duties of the airspace control authority, the area air defense commander, and/or the space coordinating authority as designated.

- Implement a personnel recovery plan for their own forces.

Figure III-6. Multinational Force Air Component Commander Notional Responsibilities

(4) **Airspace Control.** The primary purpose of airspace control is to increase combat effectiveness by promoting the safe, effective, and flexible use of airspace with minimal restraint imposed on the users. International agreements, enemy and friendly force structures, deployments and resupply operations, commanders' concepts and operations, and operating environments such as foreign countries, the high seas, and amphibious objective areas will necessitate different specific arrangements for airspace control.

(a) **Responsibility.** The responsibility for airspace control rests with the MNFC, who normally designates an airspace control authority (ACA) to coordinate the airspace control activities for multinational operations. The broad responsibilities of the ACA include establishing, coordinating, and integrating the use of the airspace control area. Subject to the authority and approval of the MNFC, the ACA develops broad policies and procedures for airspace control and for the coordination required among nations' forces.

(b) When operating outside of a combat environment and within the borders of another sovereign nation, the ACA may perform coordination rather than control over the airspace. In those situations, the ACA needs to establish an effective relationship with the HN airspace authority. Also, in addition to increasing effectiveness, the HN interests are likely to include safe domestic civil aviation, efficient commercial aviation, and international overflight rights. Integrating airspace control efforts will have a positive impact on the overall relationship between the HN and the MNF.

(c) The ACA establishes an airspace control system that is responsive to the needs of the MNFC, integrates the MNF airspace control system with that of the HN, and coordinates and deconflicts user requirements. Centralized direction by the ACA does not imply command authority over any assets. Matters on which the ACA is unable to obtain agreement are referred to the MNFC for resolution. The responsibilities of ACA and MNFACC are interrelated and should normally be assigned to one individual. If this is not possible, the ACA staff should be colocated with the MNFACC staff.

See JP 3-52, Joint Airspace Control, *for specific information on US joint operations and AJP-3.3.5,* Airspace Control, *for specific information on NATO operations.*

(5) **Air Defense.** Air and missile defense operations must be coordinated with other operations, both on and over land and sea. The MNFC normally designates an area air defense commander (AADC) to integrate the MNF's defensive effort. The responsibilities of the MNFACC, AADC, and ACA are interrelated and are normally assigned to one individual. When the situation dictates, the MNFC may designate a separate AADC and/or ACA. In those combined operations where separate commanders are required and designated, close coordination is essential for unity of effort, prevention of friendly fire, and deconfliction of combined air operations.

See JP 3-01, Countering Air and Missile Threats, *for details on air and missile defense operations.*

(6) **Sustainment.** The following factors significantly influence sustainability during air operations:

(a) Available air frames (fixed and rotary wing).

(b) Landing fields/air base support infrastructure.

(c) Weather.

(d) Maintenance.

(e) Supply.

(f) Storage facilities.

(g) Transportation.

(h) Technical support and requirements.

(i) Common sourcing of support.

(j) Secure LOCs.

(k) Medical support requirements and capabilities.

See JP 4-08, Logistics in Support of Multinational Operations, *for more information on sustainment.*

d. **Space Operations**

(1) MNFCs depend upon and exploit the advantages of space-based capabilities. Available space capabilities are normally limited to already deployed assets and established priorities for space system resources. Space systems offer global coverage and the potential for real time and near real time support to military operations. United States Strategic Command (USSTRATCOM), through the Joint Functional Component Command for Space, enables commands to access various space capabilities and systems. As situations develop, priorities for space services may change to aid the MNFC in assessing the changing environment. Most important, MNFCs and their components need to anticipate "surge" space-based capabilities needed for future phases due to the long lead times to reprioritize or acquire additional capability.

(2) **Space Integration into MNF Operations.** MNFs will have many of the same requirements for space support as do US forces. Sharing of intelligence products is controlled according to intelligence guidelines. Commercial imagery in its native state (unannotated) may facilitate information sharing with other MNFs. Weather data is also readily available to share, as is global positioning system navigation support. Providing warning of and defense against attack from all classes of ballistic missiles is important because it helps build trust among MNFs. USSTRATCOM is responsible for assisting in development of missile warning architectures and providing this information to MNFs in a process called "shared early warning."

(3) **Space Coordinating Authority (SCA).** During campaigns or major operations, the SCA gathers operational requirements that may be satisfied by space capabilities and facilitates the use of established processes by joint force staffs to plan and conduct space operations. The SCA coordinates with each MNF component and ally to reduce redundancy among, and interference between, space operations, as well as conflicting support requests reaching USSTRATCOM. The MNFC should consider the mission, nature and duration of the operation, preponderance of space force capabilities, and the C2 (including reachback) in designating SCA. MNF coordinating authority is normally retained at the MNF level, but may be delegated to a component.

For additional information on space operations, see JP 3-14, Space Operations.

e. **Information Operations (IO).** Information is a strategic, operational, and tactical resource, vital to national security. Military operations at all levels depend on information and information systems for many simultaneous and integrated activities. IO integrate the employment, during military operations, of information-related capabilities (IRCs) in concert with other lines of operation to influence, disrupt, corrupt, or usurp the decision making of adversaries and potential adversaries while protecting our own.

(1) Multinational IO depend on a systemic understanding of the information environment, cooperative arrangements with the aims of full coordination and integration of options, and flexibility and adaptability to mission and situation requirements. The development of capabilities, TTP, plans, intelligence, and communications support applicable to IO must begin early so that IRCs can be integrated into the overall operation or

campaign plan. This development also requires coordination with the responsible DOD components and partner nations. Coordination with allies above the JFC/MNFC level is normally effected within existing defense arrangements, including bilateral arrangements. DOD, through the Joint Staff, coordinates US positions on all IO matters discussed bilaterally or in multinational organizations to encourage interoperability and compatibility in fulfilling common requirements. Direct discussions regarding multinational operations in a specific theater are the responsibility of the GCC.

(2) **The Multinational IO Cell**

(a) When the JFC is also the MNFC, the joint force staff should be augmented by planners and subject matter experts from the MNF. All MNF member nations should be represented in the IO cell in positions to contribute, when possible, to the development of the IO plan. IO planners should seek to accommodate the requirements of the MNF with the goal of using all the available IO resources. Direct representation enables multinational IO assets to be used efficiently and ensures that the multinational IO plan is coordinated with all other aspects of the multinational operation.

1. Each nation has various resources to provide both classified and unclassified information to a particular IO activity. To maximize the benefits of IRCs, all nations must be willing to share appropriate information to accomplish the assigned mission. However, all MNF members should understand that each nation is obliged to protect information that it cannot share with other MNF nations.

2. Information sharing arrangements in formal alliances, to include US participation in UN missions, are worked out as part of alliance protocols. Information sharing arrangements in ad hoc multinational operations where coalitions are working together on a short-notice mission, must be created during the establishment of the coalition.

For more information, see JP 3-13, Information Operations. *For NATO-specific doctrine, see AJP-3.10,* Allied Joint Doctrine for Information Operations.

(b) In the case where the JFC is not the MNFC, it may be necessary for the JFC to brief the MNFC and staff on the advantages of IO as a part of military strategy to achieve US and MNF goals. The JFC should propose organizing a multinational IO cell. If this is not acceptable to the MNFC, the JFC should assume responsibility for using IO as a part of military strategy within the joint force to support US and MNF objectives.

(3) **Multinational IO Planning.** Planning IO to support multinational operations is more difficult because of complex approval and security issues, differences in the level of training of involved forces, interoperability of equipment, and language barriers.

(a) How to plan multinational IO is the prerogative of the MNFC. The size, composition, and mission of the MNF, as well as diplomatic considerations, may influence how multinational IO is planned. Coordination at the IO cell level with detailed planning at the individual element level would give multinational IO planning the most consistency with US IO planning procedures.

(b) The multinational IO plan should directly and demonstrably support the objectives of the MNFC. This is particularly important when joint force planners are attempting to acquaint a non-US MNFC with the advantages of IO as a part of military strategy.

(c) The subordinate JFC may undertake planning and execution of independent IO in support of multinational objectives.

See CJCSI 6510.01, Information Assurance (IA) and Support to Computer Network Defense (CND).

(4) Military information support operations (MISO) provides the commander with the ability to convey selected information and indicators to foreign audiences to influence their emotions, motives, objective reasoning, and ultimately the behavior of foreign governments, organizations, groups, and individuals. The purpose of MISO is to induce or reinforce foreign attitudes and behavior favorable to the originator's objectives. MISO should be incorporated into all multinational operations. The MNFC should ensure that all MISO, regardless of national origin, are coordinated. MISO planning must begin early, preferably before deployment, to prepare a population for the arrival of MNFs and develop communication channels that can be used from day one of the operation. A detailed analysis of a country's culture, political climate, and military organization can help the MNFC to effectively apply MISO to communicate policy, provide information, and persuade groups to cooperate with friendly forces. US MISO are approved in US channels regardless of the composition of the MNF chain of command. Many NATO and Partnership for Peace nations still use the term psychological operations.

See JP 3-13.2, Military Information Support Operations, *for additional information.*

f. **Cyberspace Operations**

(1) **Cyberspace** is a global domain within the information environment consisting of the interdependent network of information technology infrastructures and resident data, including the Internet, telecommunications networks, computer systems, space-based resources, and embedded processors and controllers. Cyberspace uses electronics and the electromagnetic spectrum to create, store, modify, and exchange data via networked systems. Cyberspace operations is the employment of cyberspace capabilities where the primary purpose is to achieve objectives in or through cyberspace.

(2) Nations' understanding of the role of cyberspace in military operations continues to evolve. Operating capabilities, philosophies, and national limitations on cyberspace activities in support of military operations are changing at a tempo that affects ongoing MNF operations as well as the planning of potential future ones. Mutually beneficial national interests usually govern a contributing nation's involvement in MNF cyberspace operations. The level of multinational network and other cyberspace operations integration is directly influenced by the partnerships or agreements made with contributing nations.

(3) Multinational operations are becoming the norm for military operations, making intelligence and information sharing with partner nations increasingly important. Cyberspace connectivity, security, and assurance are essential for the multinational and HN forces' effective mutual support during operations. Cyberspace interoperability issues should also be considered in light of the information assurance requirement.

(4) Cyberspace efforts by all adversaries may include attempts to penetrate US, MNF, and HN networks to collect data on forces and systems, or to create denial or manipulation effects. Close coordination and partnership between forces, public-private stakeholders, and multinational partners will be required to rapidly develop and maintain cyberspace SA.

15. Stability Operations

a. Stability operations are a core US military mission that helps to establish order that advances US interests and values. The immediate goal often is to provide the local populace with security, restore essential services, and meet humanitarian needs. The long-term goal is to help develop indigenous capacity for securing essential services, a viable market economy, rule of law, democratic institutions, and a robust civil society.

b. Stability operations are necessary to ensure that the threat (military and/or political) is reduced to a manageable level that can be controlled by the potential civil authority or, in noncombat situations, to ensure that the situation leading to the original crisis does not reoccur or that its effects are mitigated.

c. Stability operations that support transition and reconstruction efforts primarily support USG departments and agencies, IGOs, and NGOs to restore civil authority, rebuild the infrastructure, and reestablish commerce, education, and public utilities.

d. Joint force planning and operations conducted prior to commencement of hostilities should establish a sound foundation for operations in the stabilize and enable civil authority phases. JFCs should anticipate and address how to fill the power vacuum created when sustained combat operations wind down. Accomplishing this task should ease the transition to operations in the stabilize phase and shorten the path to the national strategic end state and handover to another authority. Considerations include:

(1) Limiting the damage to key infrastructure and services.

(2) Establishing the intended disposition of captured leadership and demobilized military and paramilitary forces.

(3) Providing for the availability of cash.

(4) Identifying and managing potential stabilize phase enemies.

(5) Determining the proper force mix (e.g., combat, military police, CA, engineer, medical, multinational).

(6) Availability of HN law enforcement, health service delivery, and force health protection (FHP) resources.

(7) Securing key infrastructure nodes and facilitating HN law enforcement and first responder services.

(8) Developing and disseminating multinational communication-related themes to suppress potential new enemies and promote new governmental authority.

For specific details on stability operations, see JP 3-0, Joint Operations; *JP 3-07,* Stability Operations; *DODI 3000.05,* Stability Operations; *NSPD-44,* Management of Interagency Efforts Concerning Reconstruction and Stabilization; *JP 3-24,* Counterinsurgency Operations; *and JP 4-02,* Health Services.

16. Special Operations

a. SOF provide the MNTF with a wide range of specialized military capabilities and responses. SOF can provide specific assistance in the area of assessment, liaison, and training of host country forces within the MNTF OA. Special operations responsibility will normally be assigned to a multinational force special operations component commander (MNFSOCC) or to a TF within the MNF command structure. The TF may be made up of SOF from one nation or multiple nations depending on the situation and the interoperability factors of the nations involved. Figure III-7 contains a representative sample of MNFSOCC responsibilities.

b. SOF may deploy ahead of the multinational operations to evaluate capability of foreign units and identify training necessary to integrate them into the overall plan. This capability is enhanced by routine interaction of SOF with foreign military units including, for example, combat aviation advisory support. SOF can make use of their language and cultural capabilities to liaise with multinational units as needed. SOF can provide training to HN forces or MNFs to overcome existing shortfalls identified during the assessment.

For specific details on special operations, see JP 3-05, Special Operations, *and JP 3-22,* Foreign Internal Defense. For NATO-specific doctrine, see AJP-3.5(A), *Allied Joint Doctrine for Special Operations.*

17. Civil Affairs Support

CA provides the military commander with expertise on the civil component of the OE. The commander uses CA capabilities to analyze and influence the local populace through specific processes and dedicated resources and personnel. As part of the commander's CMO, CA conducts operations nested within the overall mission and intent. CA contributes significantly to ensuring the legitimacy and credibility of the mission. The key to understanding the role of CA is recognizing the importance of leveraging each relationship between the command and every individual, group, and organization in the OE to create a desired effect and achieve the overall objectives. CA units can provide support to non-US units in multinational operations. Planners coordinating CA support must realize the

---

Multinational Force Special Operations Component Commander Notional Responsibilities

- Advise the multinational force commander (MNFC) on the proper employment of special operations forces (SOF) and assets.

- Plan and coordinate special operations (SO) and employ designated SOF in support of the MNFC's concept of operations.

- Issue planning guidance.

- Analyze various courses of action.

- Coordinate the conduct of SO with other component commanders and forces assigned to or supporting the MNFC.

- Evaluate the results of SO.

- Synchronize sustainment for SOF.

- Establish a combat identification standing operating procedure and other directives based on MNFC guidance.

- Function as a supported/supporting commander, as directed by the MNFC.

- Focus operational-level functions and their span of control.

- Develop and support selected information operations efforts.

- Responsible for a personnel recovery plan covering their forces and should establish a personnel recovery coordination center.

Figure III-7. Multinational Force Special Operations Component Commander Notional Responsibilities

majority of US CA units are in the Reserve Component and consider the mobilization timelines and requirements to access these forces to support multinational operations.

a. Incorporating liaison and coordination procedures into concept plans (CONPLANs) and OPLANs (especially in a CMO annex) will facilitate proper education, training, and exercising between military and civilian personnel and assist the commander in transitioning responsibility, when directed, to the appropriate organizations upon mission completion. One method to facilitate unified action and conduct on-site interagency coordination for CMO is to establish a CMOC. The CMOC serves as the primary coordination interface for the Armed Forces of the United States and humanitarian organizations, IGOs, NGOs, multinational military forces, and other civilian agencies of the USG. The CMOC facilitates continuous coordination among the key participants with regard to CMO and CA operations from local levels to international levels within a given OA, and develops, manages, and analyzes the civil inputs to the common operational picture, but is not an operations center in the same sense as a tactical operations center or joint operations center. Army CA units (down to company level) have a standing CMOC capability and can form the core of the MNF CMOC.

See JP 3-57, Civil-Military Operations, *for further information.*

---

b. **NATO CIMIC.** Within NATO, CMO is often referred to as CIMIC. CIMIC refers to "the resources and arrangements which support the relationship between commanders and the national authorities, civil and military, and civil populations in an area where military forces are or plan to be employed." Such arrangements include cooperation with nongovernmental or international agencies, organizations, and authorities.

c. Generally, CIMIC expands on CA activities that refer primarily to support of the civil component of the OE in order to influence the civilian environment in support of the armed forces. While CIMIC and CA activities often overlap on the ground, there is a clear doctrinal difference in scope. While CA encompasses activities undertaken to establish and maintain relations between military forces and civil authorities as well as the general population, CIMIC focuses on humanitarian need and provides guidance for how to interact with civilian actors (civil authorities, local populations, international organizations, and NGOs) to effectively complete the objectives of a humanitarian mission. CA, by contrast, focuses on military needs and provides suggestions for how to gain the support of civilians for the military mission. Whereas CIMIC and CA forces have similar roles, the CA forces have a much broader function and different focus than most CIMIC organizations. Despite these noticeable distinctions between CA and CIMIC, the two approaches share sufficient common ground to be compatible.

d. CIMIC doctrine involves aspects of both CMO and interorganizational coordination as described in joint doctrine. Additionally, CIMIC teams are comprised of a mixture of military and civilian members, much like a provincial reconstruction team.

See AJP-3.4.9, Allied Joint Doctrine for Civil-Military Cooperation, *for additional information.*

NORTH ATLANTIC TREATY ORGANIZATION
CIVIL-MILITARY COOPERATION (CIMIC)

Thirteen North Atlantic Treaty Organization (NATO) nations directly commanded twenty-seven active provincial reconstruction teams (PRTs) simultaneously engaged in a variety of sixty-four CIMIC operations and projects scattered throughout Afghanistan. Coordinating this significant presence of widely dispersed international assistance personnel is one of the tasks of NATO's Multinational CIMIC Group (MNCG) Headquarters established in 2009. MNCG is able to engage CIMIC activities to support NATO and multinational operations, to enhance the effectiveness of military operations and serve as an essential forum for CIMIC consultations, planning staff, and a center of expertise. MNCG's Deployable Module or implementation detachments provide the permanent specialist core able to coordinate any kind of CIMIC effort as well as provide consultancy and advice to the force commander.

MNCG ensures that although flexible and different from each other, all PRTs share the same NATO CIMIC mission and the same operational/strategic

---

NATO CIMIC concept allowing them to operate independently in the field while pursuing the common goals of investing in reconstruction of the most critical areas of education, health, agriculture, small infrastructure, security, and governance, while limiting or eliminating duplication of effort and increasing cooperation between organizations. During a 12-month period:

In the town of Ala Chapan outside Mazar-e Sharif, German International Security Assistance Force (ISAF) CIMIC members working with the German charity organization "German Forces helping children of the developing world" completed construction and opened a high school capable of serving 1,600 Afghan students.

In Herat, an Italian team delivered educational supplies and a monetary contribution donated by the Udine Italy Rotary Club to a 500-student Herat children's school.

In Lashkar Gah, new medical equipment donated by Estonia was delivered to the Bost Hospital by Estonian CIMIC officers operating out of the Helmand PRT base.

In Logar Province, the Czech PRT continued to assist Afghan National Security Forces by training members of the Afghan National Police in basic policing skills and knowledge.

At Shamail Daria village, Spanish ISAF doctors held a medical clinic arranged by the Spanish CIMIC unit in a building constructed by the Spanish Cooperation for Development Agency.

Greek authorities provided significant funding for the Hungarian PRT implementing CIMIC civilian development projects in Afghanistan's Baghlan Province aimed at training, education, and health with specific focus on improving the situation of Afghan women and creating job opportunities.

Various Sources

18. Joint Fires

a. Joint fires address the integration of all joint lethal and nonlethal capabilities to create effects. Joint fires are delivered during the employment of forces from two or more components in coordinated action to produce desired effects in support of a common objective. Fires typically produce destructive effects, but some ways and means (such as electronic attack) can be employed with little or no associated physical destruction. This function encompasses the fires produced by a number of tasks (or missions, actions, and processes) including:

(1) Conducting joint targeting.

(2) Providing joint fire support.

(3) Countering air and missile threats.

(4) Interdicting enemy capabilities.

(5) Conducting strategic attack.

(6) Employing IRCs.

(7) Assessing the results of employing fires.

b. Integrating and synchronizing planning, execution, and assessment is pivotal to the success of effective joint fires. Understanding the objectives, intentions, capabilities, and limitations of all actors within the OE enables the use of joint, interagency, and multinational means to accomplish tasks and create effects.

c. Effective fire support coordination in multinational operations may require additional efforts due to differing national priorities and the risk of friendly fire, civilian casualties, and collateral damage. To maximize the fires of the MNF and to minimize the possibility of friendly fire, the MNFC should ensure that fire support coordination throughout the MNF is developed. These special arrangements may include communications and language requirements, liaison personnel, and interoperability procedures. Standard operating procedures should be established for fire support to achieve the most effective results for its use by the MNF.

See JP 3-09, Joint Fire Support, *for more details. For NATO-specific doctrine, see AJP-3.9,* Allied Joint Doctrine for Joint Targeting.

19. Electromagnetic Spectrum Management

Effective electromagnetic spectrum management is essential to integrate and deconflict MNF use of the electromagnetic spectrum for communications, C2, sensor operations, IO, electronic warfare, and force protection. The varieties of systems which partner nations may depend upon, the number of suppliers, indigenous systems that use the spectrum, and fidelity of use and interference data make electromagnetic spectrum management far more demanding in multinational operations than in joint operations.

For more information on spectrum management, refer to JP 6-01, Joint Electromagnetic Spectrum Management Operations.

20. Multinational Communications Integration

a. Multinational communications integration (MCI) is the MNFs' coordination and employment of actions, images, and words to support the achievement of participating nations' overall strategic objectives and end state. The commander of the MNF receives multinational communication strategy guidance for MCI and is responsible for integrating this guidance into all plans, operations, and actions of the MNF.

(1) MCI consists of coordinated programs, plans, themes, messages, and products synchronized with the actions of all instruments of national power in an MNF at the strategic, operational, and tactical levels. MCI focuses on creating, strengthening, or preserving conditions favorable to achieve the MNF's mission. In an MNF, the key is coordinated communication integration among participating nations.

(2) The MCI should integrate all IRCs into planning activities relevant to the mission, addressing both current and future operations (see Figure III-8). This plan should minimize adverse effects on multinational operations from inaccurate media reporting/analysis, violations of OPSEC, adversary propaganda, and promulgation of disinformation and misinformation. Well-planned IRC support is important in every phase of operations.

b. The MNFs' predominant military activities that support MCI are IO, public affairs (PA), and defense support to public diplomacy (DSPD). All multinational operations (executed or not executed) should be viewed through the MCI perspectives and framework to facilitate support of strategic objectives and end state. Communication planning and synchronization guidance should be integrated into military planning and operations, documented in OPLANs, and coordinated and synchronized with USG departments and agencies and multinational partners.

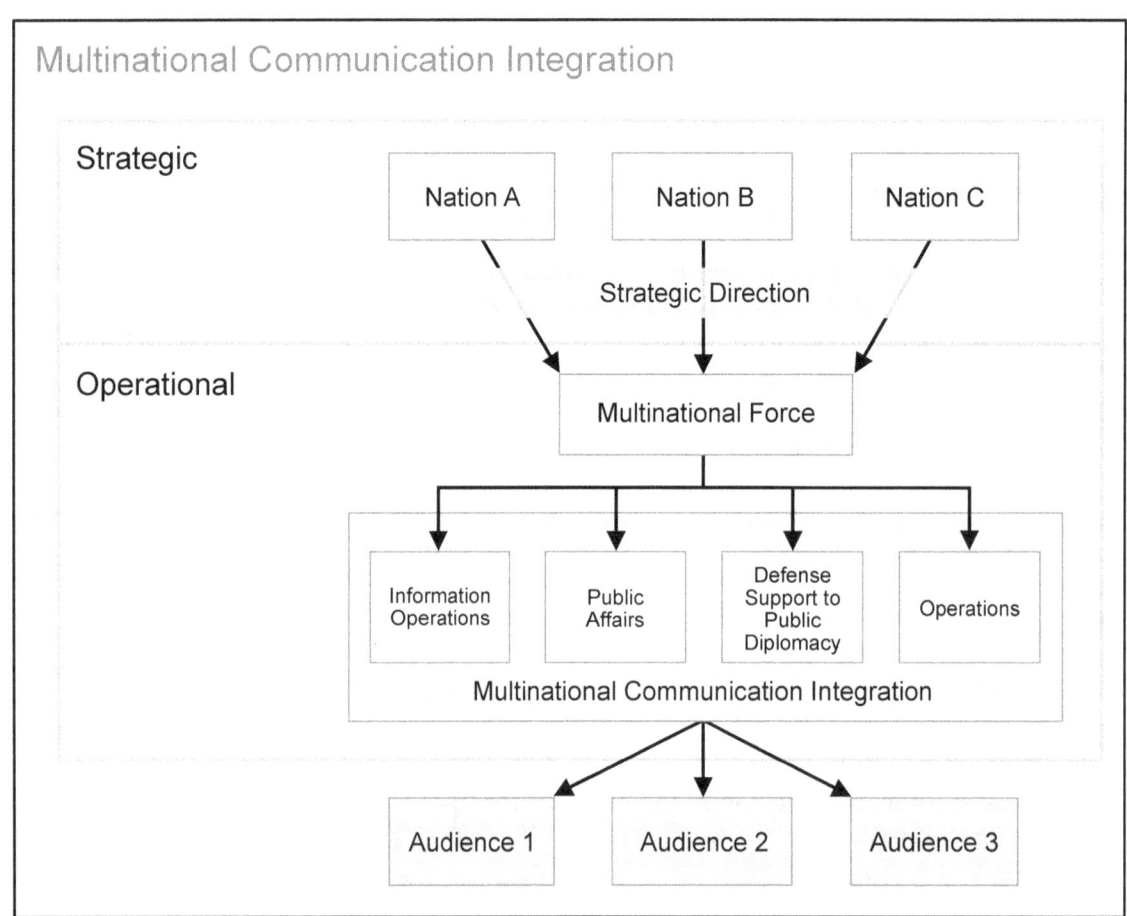

Figure III-8. Multinational Communication Integration

c. In addition to addressing MCI with partners during the mission analysis, careful and thorough planning and coordination with multinational partners is critical to ensure the messages are consistent and account for regional, cultural, and language interpretations and perceptions. However, it is also important to recognize that interagency and multinational partners may have their own goals and objectives, not all of which will be revealed to the MNF, which may result in considerable challenges to the MCI effort.

Refer to JP 1, Doctrine for the Armed Forces of the United States; *JP 3-0,* Joint Operations; *JP 3-13,* Information Operations; *JP 5-0,* Joint Operation Planning; *and JP 3-61,* Public Affairs, *for more information on strategic guidance and the informational instrument of national power, IO, and PA.*

d. The nature of each nation's decision to participate in a multinational operation will influence what they communicate to their population about their involvement. The communication activities of each nation in the operation will reach audiences in the other countries and serve to either support or undermine the objectives of the MNF and those of the individual participating nations.

21. Public Affairs

a. US PA planners should work closely with those individuals from other countries who conduct public information activities to ensure that the planning of each nation takes into consideration the objectives of the others involved.

b. Commanders at all levels should anticipate media coverage for multinational operations. They should plan to support the media in their assigned OAs IAW the PA guidance of the OPLAN. Media coverage of US operations is generally a key component of the PA strategy and coverage should be facilitated to support it. PA advises the MNFC on the possible impact of military operations and activities within the public information realm.

(1) The speed and methods with which people and organizations can collect and convey information to the public makes it possible for the world populace to quickly become aware of an incident. Internet sites, social media, text messages, and cellular telephones are some of the means through which potential adversaries engage audiences worldwide in the information environment. This instantaneous, unfiltered and often incomplete, intentionally biased, or factually incorrect information provided via satellite and the Internet makes planning and effective execution of PA essential.

(2) PA plans should provide for open, independent reporting and anticipate and respond to media queries. These plans should provide the maximum disclosure allowed with minimum delay and create an environment between the MNF and reporters that encourages balanced coverage of operations. Additionally, the MNF PA plan should make use of social media to get ahead of the narrative, explaining the MNF operations and using social media as a means of unclassified coordinating with NGOs and HN agencies.

(3) In most multinational operations one or more centers will be established to support the media. Although the title may vary by operation depending on the command

> "Fewer than 30 reporters accompanied the entire invasion force to Normandy, France, on 6 June 1944. In contrast, more than 500 journalists appeared within hours to cover combat operations in Grenada in 1983 and Panama in 1989. At the beginning of Operation DESERT STORM in 1991, more than 1,600 news media and support personnel were present, and some 1,500 reported on hurricane relief operations in Florida in 1992. Reporters provided live television and radio coverage of the night amphibious landing that marked the beginning of Operation RESTORE HOPE in Somalia in 1992 and the end of the United Nations operation during Operation UNITED SHIELD in 1995. More than 1,700 media representatives covered the initial phases of peacekeeping operations in the American sector of Bosnia in 1996."
>
> **Major Barry Veneble, US Army, *Military Review*, January-February 2002**

structure, these centers are established to serve as the focal point for the interface between the military and the media during operations.

(4) Responsibilities for establishing media ground rules and credentialing media are developed and implemented through appropriate multinational command and staff channels. Media outlets owned entirely or in part by governments or citizens of rival states might not receive the same considerations as those working for outlets owned by governments or citizens of friendly nations. Additionally, noncredentialed journalists may not be given the same access to a combat zone as those who have credentials. They should be encouraged to register at the appropriate information center.

(5) Credentialing is not intended to be a control measure or means to restrict certain media outlets from access. It is primarily a method of validating individuals as journalists and providing them with information that enhances their ability to report on activities within the OA. Additionally, media must be credentialed to ensure that they have official status under the Geneva Conventions in the event of capture. Others covering military operations without such credentials should be encouraged to register at the appropriate facility.

For US-specific doctrine, see JP 3-61, Public Affairs, *for additional details. For NATO-specific doctrine, see AJP-3.10,* Allied Joint Doctrine for Information Operations.

22. Multinational Logistics

a. Successful multinational logistic operations are governed by several unique principles. First, multinational logistic operations are a collective responsibility of participating nations and the MNFC, although nations are inherently responsible for supporting their forces. Nations are highly reluctant to give MNFCs complete authority for logistics. Nevertheless, a second principle is that MNFCs should be given sufficient authority over logistic resources to ensure that the force is supported in the most efficient and effective manner. Third, cooperation and coordination are necessary among participating nations and forces, which should make use of multinational logistic support arrangements in order to reduce the logistic footprint in the OA. Finally, synergy results from the use of multinational integrated logistic support; to ensure this, the MNFC must have visibility of the logistic activity during the operation.

b. Multinational operations are highly political. Generally, nations are reluctant to commit forces early. In some MNFs, formal advance planning is considered too sensitive for sharing. Thus, US logistic planners must work closely with partner nations to the extent possible in coordinating national plans to support political decisions. Obtaining early knowledge of the organic logistic support capabilities of forces provided by participating nations and identifying the means to support their needs will be critical to effectively supporting the total force.

c. Several major considerations affect US logistics participation in multinational operations. First, US forces and logistic resources may be placed under the OPCON or TACON of a foreign MNFC based on the transfer of authority delegated by the US. This does not imply that MNFCs have authoritative control of US logistics resources or capabilities. OPCON as defined in JP 1, *Doctrine for the Armed Forces of the United States,* does not, in and of itself, include authoritative direction for logistics or matters of administration. Second, US laws affect the exchange of logistic support between US forces and those of other nations as well as with HNs; US commanders must be aware of these legal considerations. Third, consultation, cooperation, and coordination between US commanders and other nations, multinational HQ, and forces is essential to achieve unity of effort in providing logistic support. The use of centralized coordination centers in such areas as movement control, operational contract support, civil engineering, customs and border clearance, and medical support can assist US commanders in effectively supporting US forces. Finally, use of multinational logistic support arrangements, coupled with modern technology and concepts, is important for synchronized deployment and timely sustainment of an MNF with a reduced logistic footprint in the OA. Advances in such areas as information technology, joint deployment, and theater distribution systems can benefit both the planning and execution of multinational logistics activities and enhance US and MNF military capability.

Additional guidance on multinational logistics can be found in JP 4-0, Joint Logistics; *JP 4-08,* Logistics in Support of Multinational Operations; *JP 4-09,* Distribution Operations; *and JP 4-10,* Operational Contract Support. *For specific NATO doctrine, see AJP-4 and other AJPs in the 4 Series.*

23. Chemical, Biological, Radiological, and Nuclear Operations

a. Operations in chemical, biological, radiological, and nuclear (CBRN) environments present a unique challenge, and one that is compounded by the prospect of performing them under the auspices of multinational operations. Nations have unique equipment and procedures for surviving and operating in CBRN environments.

b. An adversary's CBRN capabilities or the existence of significant quantities of toxic industrial material in the OE can have a profound impact on US and multinational objectives, the CONOPS, and supporting actions, and therefore must be taken into account.

See JP 3-11, Operations in Chemical, Biological, Radiological, and Nuclear (CBRN) Environments, *for CBRN planning considerations.*

24. Counterdrug Operations

a. Counterdrug (CD) operations are inherently interagency and/or multinational in nature. DOD supports the USG lead agencies for both domestic and international CD operations, so military planning requires coordination and collaboration with relevant agencies and multinational partners. This helps ensure the effective integration of supporting military forces and equipment, which often are the primary capabilities required for the CD operation. Military planners must understand that some of the agencies and multinational organizations that lead or might become involved in CD operations will have different goals, capabilities, limitations (such as policy and resource constraints), standards, and operational philosophies.

b. Coordination and collaboration can be accomplished by integrating the efforts of military, civilian agency, and multinational planners early in the planning process. Military commanders who support CD operations must ensure that interagency and multinational planners clearly understand military capabilities, requirements, operational limitations, liaison, and legal considerations and that military planners understand the nature of the relationship and the types of support they can provide. Robust liaison facilitates understanding, coordination, and mission accomplishment.

See JP 3-07.4, Joint Counterdrug Operations, *for more information. Also refer to JP 3-08,* Interorganizational Coordination During Joint Operations, *for interagency and multinational considerations.*

25. Personnel Recovery

a. Personnel recovery (PR) is the sum of military, diplomatic, and civil efforts to prepare for and execute the recovery and reintegration of isolated personnel. PR may occur through three options (diplomatic, civil, or military) or through any combination of these options. In multinational operations, PR does not include noncombatant evacuation operations (NEOs), peacetime search and rescue (SAR), or salvage operations.

b. The MNFC must make a careful assessment of each MNF nation's PR capability and procedures. Normally, each nation and/or component is responsible for conducting its own PR missions. However, participants may possess a variety of PR methods ranging from civil SAR to dedicated combat SAR. Therefore, the MNFC may designate an individual or establish an organization and procedures to coordinate this mission among all participants.

c. **Personnel Recovery Coordination Center (PRCC).** The MNFC should create a PRCC to act as the MNF focal point for all personnel and equipment ready to perform PR within the AO. The actual name of the PRCC will be based on the arrangement of the participating nations and could be joint or multinational. Functions of the PRCC include:

(1) Coordinate PR operations both within the MNF and with external organizations.

(2) Advise the MNFC or designated component commander on PR incidents and requests.

(3) Coordinate requests for augmentation to support recovery operations as required.

d. PR operations may extend across national lines of responsibility. Operational flexibility, interoperability, and multisystem redundancy are the primary factors in successful PR operations. Commanders should know the PR capabilities available to maximize unified action, achieve economy of force, and enhance SA to enable those most capable of executing the five PR execution tasks: report, locate, support, recover, and reintegrate.

See JP 3-50, Personnel Recovery, *for information on how to organize a comprehensive joint/combined PR network.*

SECTION C. OTHER CONSIDERATIONS

26. Host-Nation Support

a. **HNS will often be critical to the success of a multinational operation.** In general, centralized coordination of HNS planning and execution will help ensure that HNS resources are allocated most effectively to support the MNF's priorities. The more limited HNS resources are in the OA, the greater the requirement for centralized management.

b. NATO doctrine recognizes the importance of centralized HNS coordination and gives NATO commanders the authority to:

(1) Prioritize HNS requirements.

(2) Negotiate HNS agreements, on behalf of nations, with an HN.

(3) Coordinate HNS allocation with "sending" nations and an HN.

c. In US-led multinational operations, nations typically negotiate their own HNS agreements. Nevertheless, participating nations should coordinate their HNS arrangements with the MNFC, who in turn should coordinate HNS allocation with the HN. The MNFC should involve participating nations in the negotiation of either commonly worded separate bilateral target audiences or a single agreement applicable to the entire MNTF.

d. **Host-Nation Support Coordination Cell (HNSCC).** To assist the MNFC in HNS coordination activities, an HNSCC may be established. One of the most important functions of the HNSCC is to assist the MNFC and legal counsel in developing technical arrangements (TAs) that involve sustainment matters such as infrastructure, financial management, purchasing and operational contract support, engineering, environment, hazardous material storage, landing and port fees, medical operations and support, border customs, tariffs, and real estate.

(1) **Staffing.** The HNSCC should be staffed with specialists familiar with developing and executing HNS agreements. In addition, consideration should be given to including representatives of the HN within the HNSCC to:

(a) Facilitate coordination and identification of resources for potential use by the MNTF.

(b) Provide interpretation and translation services to the HNSCC staff.

(2) **Information Requirements.** In order to effectively plan and coordinate HNS allocation, the HNSCC needs up-to-date information on HNS logistic capabilities and ongoing HNS allocation to MNTF contingents throughout the operation. To ensure that it receives such information, the HNSCC must maintain close contact with the HN and with MNTF contingents.

(3) **Coordinating Activities.** In conducting its operations, the HNSCC coordinates closely with appropriate CMOC organizations, the multinational joint logistics center, and the HN's representatives.

e. HNS is generally furnished IAW an agreement negotiated prior to the start of an operation. HNS agreements are commonly established through diplomatic channels in bilateral and multilateral agreements with the HN. These are normally umbrella-type agreements that are augmented to support contingencies by TAs detailing the specific support to be provided and the type/amount of reimbursement.

f. During crises, it may be necessary for the US GCC to request authority to negotiate bilateral HNS agreements for the purpose of providing logistic assistance to other nations. Such negotiations are conducted in coordination with the Joint Staff, the Office of the Secretary of Defense, and DOS, and in compliance with applicable DODDs. Alternatively, the MNFC may be authorized to negotiate HNS agreements on behalf of force contributing nations, with their prior concurrence. This approach, which NATO doctrine endorses, simplifies and streamlines the process and reduces the amount of time required to put such agreements into place.

g. **Available HNS Infrastructure.** Analysis of the physical infrastructure in the HN is critical to understanding force sustainability. MNTF logistic planners should evaluate what facilities and services (such as government, law enforcement, sanitation, power, fuel, and medical support) exist as viable support for local consumption and support of coalition forces.

(1) First, assess the ability of the HN to receive MNTF personnel and equipment (e.g., ports and airfields).

(2) Second, determine the capability of transportation systems to move forces once they arrive in theater.

(3) Third, evaluate availability of logistic support.

(4) The impact of obtaining HNS on the host country's national economy must also be considered, along with possible environmental impacts upon HNs. These must be recognized and addressed during the planning process.

(5) In addition, specific technical agreements in many areas (e.g., environmental cleanup, levying of customs duties and taxes, hazardous material and/or waste storage, transit, and disposal) may need to be developed to augment SOFAs that may have been concluded with HNs.

For more information on NATO HNS procedures, see AJP-4.5, Allied Joint Host Nation Support Doctrine and Procedures.

27. Health Services

a. The medical assets committed in support of multinational operations consist of health service delivery and FHP capabilities that span the OE from point of injury/illness to the appropriate role of care. It also includes health engagements with HN civil and military authorities in support of stability operations and building partner capacity, with the goal of assisting to reestablish or strengthen the HN infrastructure and governmental legitimacy. Components within these capabilities are essential in the execution of multinational operations. The provision of medical support to multinational operations represents a number of challenges.

(1) Unique nature of every individual operation.

(2) Differences in individual national objectives and/or restrictions for participation in operations and integration of overall mission goals.

(3) Geographic, topographic, and climatic variations as well as health threats in the OA.

(4) Numbers of individual nations involved in each operation.

(5) Variations in nation standards of health service delivery, FHP, and medical equipment.

(6) Variations in HN standards of medical care and their ability to appropriately utilize and maintain medical equipment in the absence of foreign support.

(7) Language and communications differences.

(8) Political complexity and dynamic nature of each operational scenario.

(9) Mission of medical support forces.

(10) Medical staffs face unique problems affecting the health of multinational personnel deployed on operations. Therefore, operational health services requires clearly defined and distinctive guidance.

(11) Health services plans are tailored to each operation and meet the demands of geography, individual nation's needs, language, and communication difficulties. Plans

should be capable of rapid implementation, but at the same time be flexible enough to manage rapidly changing operational demands.

(12) Every operationally deployed MNF should have a surgeon and/or chief medical officer who has direct access to the MNFC. Working in coordination with the MNF staff, they should recommend guidance and/or standards to follow in multinational operations.

(13) Each deployed national contingent that has health services personnel should have a single designated individual who has the clinical responsibility for its nation's health services matters.

b. **Health Services Standards for Multinational Operations.** To qualify to participate in the MNF (and for subsequent multinational resourced medical treatment, patient movement (PM), and personal disability compensation), national contingents and individuals allocated or contracted to multinational operations must meet the basic standards of individual health and physical fitness laid down by the surgeon and/or the staff chief medical officer.

(1) Contributing nations bear ultimate responsibility for ensuring the provision of health services to their forces allocated to multinational operations. This may be discharged in a number of ways, including agreements with other nations or the appropriate multinational planning staffs and MNFCs.

(2) **International and Theater-Level Conventions for the Treatment of the Sick and Wounded.** Health services for operations will comply with provisions of the Geneva Conventions. Persons, to include detainees, entitled under the terms of the Geneva Conventions shall, without discrimination, receive medical treatment on the basis of their clinical needs and the availability of health services resources.

(3) **Standards of Health Services.** Operational health services to MNFs must meet standards that are acceptable to all participating nations.

(4) **Estimation of Medical Risk.** Estimation of medical risk and the associated casualty rates is the responsibility of the individual nation with health services advice of the multinational operational staffs. Communication of the health risk is also vital to casualty prevention, including threat identification, predeployment health briefings, and any medical follow-up that may be required.

See JP 4-02, Health Services, for further details.

c. PM, known in some nations as a holding policy, balances the treatment capability available at each role of care against the medical assets required for moving patients. PM is the act or process of moving a sick, injured, wounded, or other person to obtain medical and/or dental care or treatment. Functions include medical regulating, patient evacuation, and en route medical care. Medical staffs face numerous challenges affecting the health of multinational personnel deployed on operations. Therefore, operational health services requires clearly defined guidance. Health services plans must be tailored to each operation and meet the demands of geography, individual national needs, language, and communication difficulties. Common health services challenges in multinational operations are shown in Figure III-9.

For further information on health services and theater PM, refer to JP 4-02, Health Services.

28. Noncombatant Evacuation Operations

a. A NEO is conducted to relocate designated noncombatants threatened in a foreign country to a place of safety. NEOs are principally conducted by US forces to evacuate US citizens, but they may be expanded to include citizens from the HN as well as citizens from other countries.

b. NEOs are often characterized by uncertainty. They may be directed without warning because of sudden changes in a country's government, reoriented diplomatic or military relations with the US, a sudden hostile threat to US citizens from elements within or external to a foreign country, or in response to a natural disaster.

c. NEO methods and timing are significantly influenced by diplomatic considerations. Under ideal circumstances there may be little or no opposition; however, commanders should anticipate opposition and plan the operation like any combat operation.

d. NEOs are similar to a raid in that the operation involves swift insertion of a force, temporary occupation of physical objectives, and ends with a planned withdrawal. It differs from a raid in that force used normally is limited to that required to protect the evacuees and the evacuation force. Forces penetrating foreign territory to conduct a NEO should be kept to the minimum consistent with mission accomplishment and the security of the force and the extraction and protection of evacuees.

e. In planning for a NEO, the chief of mission, GCC, and JFC may consider the possibility of operating with MNFs. However, the approval for US participation in a multinational NEO will come only from the US President. Normally, due to the urgency of

---

Health Services Challenges in Multinational Operations

- Difference in doctrine
- Differing stockage levels
- Logistics mobility
- Interoperability concerns
- Competition between participants for common support
- Resource limitations

Figure III-9. Health Services Challenges in Multinational Operations

the situation and severe time constraints, a NEO will not be executed by a multinational command; rather, a parallel command structure of individual JTFs executing under national command is used. Under such situations, an MNCC, established by one of the JTFs in support of all JTFs, is an option for multinational coordination of operations. Under an emergency situation involving the safety of human life or the protection of property, offers of voluntary service from other countries may be accepted prior to Presidential approval.

f. Multinational evacuations involve multiple nation diplomatic initiatives—with MNFs conducting a NEO in a supporting role. A political decision from each of the participating nations is required to conduct a NEO with an MNF. Should the political powers decide on a requirement for a multinational NEO, an initiating directive should be issued to enable detailed operational planning to commence.

For additional guidance on NEOs, refer to JP 3-68, Noncombatant Evacuation Operations. *Specific guidance on conducting NEOs within NATO is provided in AJP-3.4.2,* Allied Joint Doctrine for Noncombatant Evacuation Operations.

29. Personnel Support

Military operations now include peacekeeping, humanitarian assistance, and other actions that involve managing complex crises and contingency operations. To accomplish these missions, the Services must be prepared to operate in a multinational environment. Personnel support for multinational operations remains a national responsibility; however, CCDRs and subordinate JFCs operating as part of an MNF should establish a SOFA, memorandum of agreement (MOA), and/or MOU regarding personnel support between members of any alliance and/or coalition prior to the onset of operations that clearly define JFC command authority (OPCON, TACON, etc.) over MNF personnel, command relationships, and reporting channels.

For additional guidance on personnel support to joint operations, refer to JP 1-0, Joint Personnel Support.

30. Meteorology and Oceanography

The effective understanding of meteorology and oceanography and the application of that knowledge during mission execution significantly contributes to all successful multinational operations. The state of the atmosphere and oceans is a force multiplier or detractor, depending on the mission. Successful commanders use the environment to their advantage. In multinational operations, early planning is critical. As with all multinational operations, differences in language, techniques, data formats, and communications must be overcome prior to any operation. The MNFC should designate a senior meteorological and oceanographic (METOC) officer to coordinate METOC support to facilitate coordination of METOC forces. All forces should operate from a common METOC forecast. The senior METOC officer should also consider using and disseminating multinational METOC data when available.

See JP 3-59, Meteorological and Oceanographic Operations, *for additional details.*

31. Environmental

a. Environmental considerations should be integrated in multinational operations. To the extent practicable and consistent with mission accomplishment, commanders should take environmental factors into account during planning, execution, and conclusion of a multinational operation. Commanders should also clearly identify guidance that may be different from the normal practices of the member nations and obtain agreement from participating nations. Besides agreeing on common goals and objectives for the operation, the MNF's national component commanders should reach some understanding on environmental protection measures during the operation. Failure to accomplish this may result in misunderstandings, decreased interoperability, and a failure to develop and implement a successful environmental annex and plan for the operation. Additionally, the failure to consider environmental impacts on the HN could result in an erosion of acceptance for the MNF within the HN.

b. Environmental considerations include, but are not limited to, the following:

(1) Air pollution from ships, vehicles, aircraft, and construction machinery.

(2) Cleanup of base camps and other occupied areas to an appropriate level.

(3) Protection of endangered species and marine mammals in the OA.

(4) Environmental safety and health.

(5) Hazardous material management.

(6) Hazardous waste disposal.

(7) Medical and infectious waste management and disposal.

(8) Natural and cultural resource protection.

(9) Noise abatement, including noise from aircraft operations.

(10) Pesticide, insecticide, and herbicide management to control non-point pollution.

(11) Resource and energy conservation through pollution prevention practices.

(12) Solid waste management and disposal.

(13) Oil and hazardous substance spills prevention and controls.

(14) Water pollution from sewage, food service, and other operations.

For a further discussion of environmental considerations, refer to JP 3-34, Joint Engineer Operations.

32. Transitions

a. Transitions are critical to multinational operations. In general, transitions fall into three categories: the orderly turnover of a plan or order as it is passed to those tasked with execution of the operation (i.e., future operations to current operations); transition between the various phases of an operation or campaign (such as phase II: seize the initiative to phase III: dominate); and the transition of authority for the effort from one organization to another (i.e., JTF to MNF or MNF to IGO/HN).

b. The transition of plans to execution provides information, direction, and guidance relative to the plan or order that will help to facilitate SA. Additionally, it provides an understanding of the rationale for key decisions necessary to ensure there is a coherent shift from planning to execution. These factors coupled together are intended to maintain the intent of the CONOPS, promote unity of effort, and generate tempo. Successful transition ensures that those charged with executing an order have a full understanding of the plan. Regardless of the level of command, such a transition ensures that those who execute the order understand the commander's intent and CONOPS. Transition may be internal or external in the form of briefs or drills. Internally, transition occurs between future plans and future/current operations. Externally, transition occurs between the commander and subordinate commands.

For more information on plan transitions, see JP 5-0, Joint Operation Planning.

c. **Phases.** A phase can be characterized by the focus that is placed on it. Phases are distinct in time, space, and/or purpose from one another, but must be planned in support of each other and should represent a natural progression and subdivision of the campaign or operation (see Figure III-10). Each phase should have a set of starting conditions (that define the start of the phase) and ending conditions (that define the end of the phase). The ending conditions of one phase are the starting conditions for the next phase.

(1) Working within the phasing construct, the actual phases used will vary (compressed, expanded, or omitted entirely) with the joint campaign or operation and be determined by the MNFC. During planning, the MNFC establishes conditions, objectives, or events for transitioning from one phase to another and plans sequels and branches for potential contingencies. Phases are designed to be conducted sequentially, but some activities from a phase may begin in a previous phase and continue into subsequent phases. The MNFC adjusts the phases to exploit opportunities presented by the adversary or operational situation or to react to unforeseen conditions. A joint campaign or operation may be conducted in multiple phases simultaneously if the OA has widely varying conditions. For instance, the commander may transition to the stabilize phase in some areas while remaining in the dominate phase in those areas where the enemy has not yet capitulated. Occasionally operations may revert to a previous phase in an area where a resurgent or new enemy re-engages friendly forces.

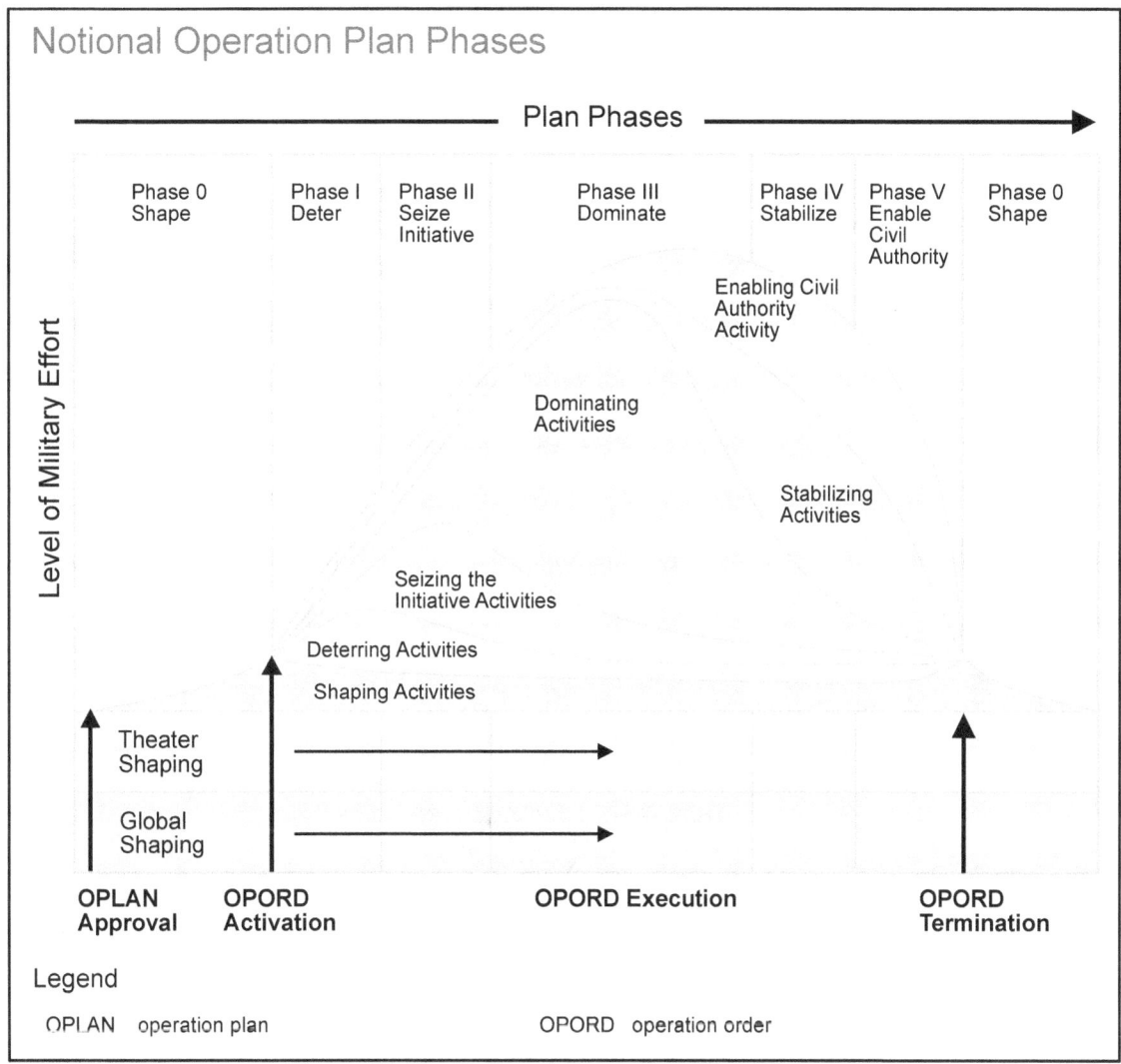

Figure III-10. Notional Operation Plan Phases

(2) Transitions between phases are designed to be distinct shifts in focus by the MNF, often accompanied by changes in command or support relationships. The activities that predominate during a given phase, however, rarely align with neatly definable breakpoints. The need to move into another phase normally is identified by assessing that a set of objectives is achieved or that the enemy has acted in a manner that requires a major change in focus for the joint force and is therefore usually event driven, not time driven. Changing the focus of the operation takes time and may require changing commander's objectives, desired effects, measures of effectiveness, priorities, command relationships, force allocation, or even the design of the OA. An example is the shift of focus from sustained combat operations in the dominate phase to a preponderance of stability operations in the stabilize and enable civil authority phases. Hostilities gradually lessen as the joint force begins to reestablish order, commerce, and local government and deters adversaries from resuming hostile actions while the US and international community take steps to establish or restore the conditions necessary for long-term stability. This challenge demands an agile shift in joint force skill sets, actions, organizational behaviors, and mental outlooks, and interorganizational coordination with a wider range of interagency and multinational

partners and other participants to provide the capabilities necessary to address the mission-specific factors.

For more information on the phasing model and details on the individual phases, refer to JP 5-0, Joint Operation Planning.

 d. **Transition of Authority.** Military operations may include transitions of authority and control among military forces, civilian agencies and organizations, and the HN as HN capacity increases (see Figure III-11). Each transition involves inherent risk. The risk is amplified when multiple transitions must be managed simultaneously or when the force must quickly conduct a series of transitions. Planning anticipates these transitions, and careful preparation and diligent execution ensure they occur without incident. Transitions are identified as decisive points on lines of effort; they typically mark a significant shift in effort and signify the gradual return to civilian oversight and control of the HN.

For more information on transitions of authority, see JP 3-07, Stability Operations.

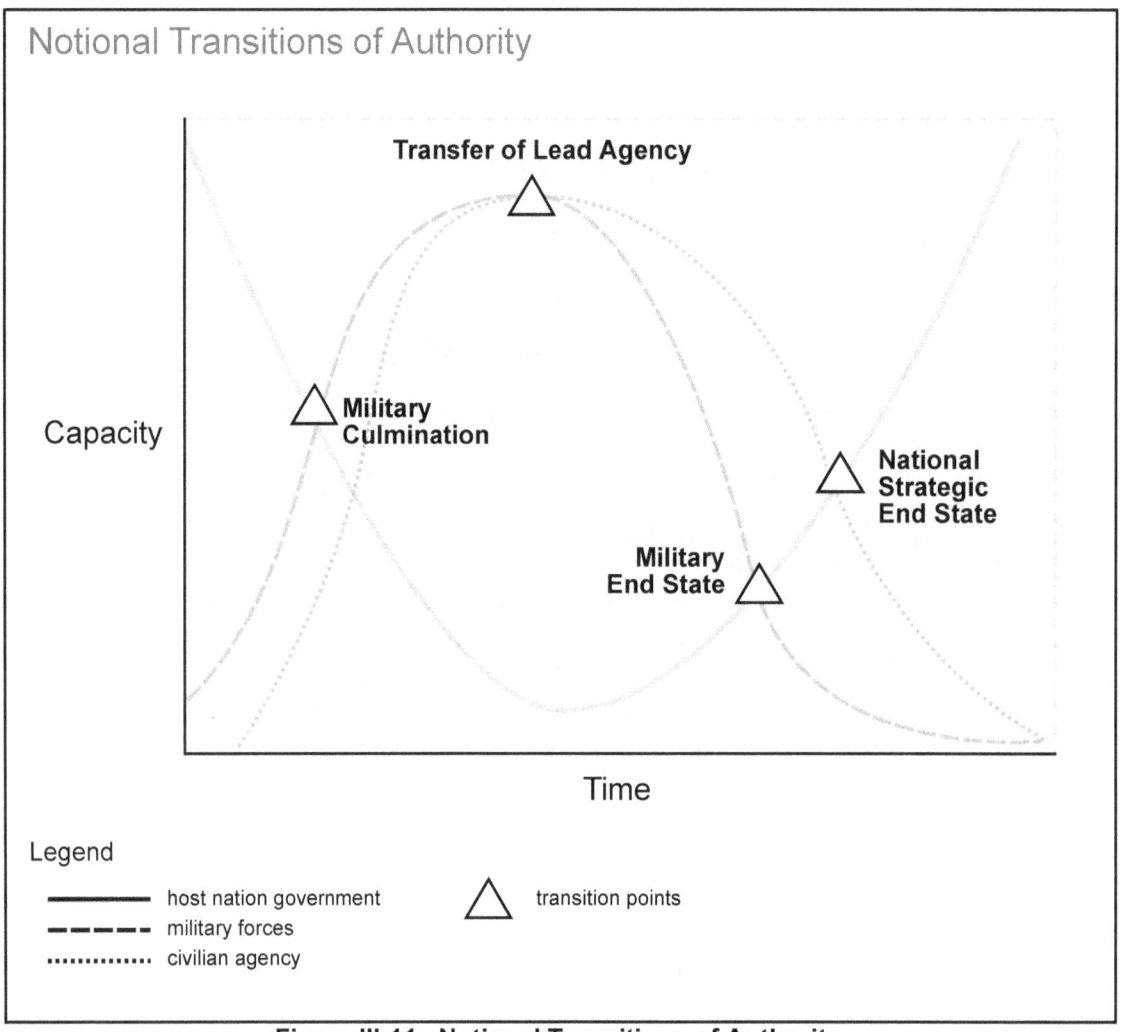

Figure III-11. Notional Transitions of Authority

33. Foreign Humanitarian Assistance

a. FHA operations, particularly in developing countries, often require the intervention and aid of various agencies from all over the world in a concerted and timely manner. As a result, operations involve dynamic information exchange, planning, and coordination. For more information, see JP 3-29, *Foreign Humanitarian Assistance.*

b. The engagement of military forces in FHA operations is based on the necessity for speed of reaction, including proximity of suitable resources to the disaster area, the scale of effort required or special skills to deal with the consequences of a humanitarian emergency/disaster. Military forces will, therefore, normally only be engaged in response to rapid onset disasters and normally at the request of humanitarian organizations through official governmental channels. The magnitude of a disaster or the threat environment may also call for military involvement in the national response. National TFs will thus provide specific support to particular requirements in response to an acknowledged humanitarian gap between the humanitarian emergency/disaster needs and relief community resources available to meet those needs. FHA operations will, therefore, normally be limited in both scope and duration.

c. FHA is not the primary role of military forces. However, military forces have an ability to quickly task organize to perform such operations and have unique capabilities that can complement the overall relief effort. In principle, military assets should be considered only when civilian capabilities have been or will become over-stretched or are unavailable, and in certain circumstances, where the use of military assets is determined to be more cost-effective in overall terms. The composition of the national TF committed in support of FHA will vary depending on the circumstances, the state of civilian coping mechanisms, and the complexity of the disaster.

d. Normally, due to the urgency of the situation, severe time constraints, and emergency relief response requirements, FHA will not be executed by a multinational command; rather, a parallel command structure of individual JTFs executing under national command is used. Under such situations an MNCC, established by one of the JTFs in support of all JTFs, is an option for multinational coordination of FHA operations. In such contingencies the MNCC also acts as a CMOC and/or CIMIC coordination center in addition to providing coordination of military support operations.

e. When military forces are involved in FHA operations their assets are provided primarily to supplement or complement the relief efforts of the affected country's civil authorities and/or of the humanitarian relief community. This support may include but is not limited to logistics, transportation, airfield management, communications, medical support, distribution of relief commodities, and security.

f. Notwithstanding specific missions, under all but exceptional circumstances, military forces deployed in support of disaster relief efforts should normally not assume leadership of the overall disaster relief. This does not preclude supporting civil C2 or providing C2 infrastructure when necessary. However, wherever possible, maximum use of established infrastructure should be made in order to preclude the national TF from becoming a hub upon which other responding agencies become reliant, thereby creating the potential for longer-term dependency and making it more difficult to redeploy at the appropriate moment. The generic military role is to support and enable the effort to relieve emergency needs until such time as disaster coping capacities no longer require military support. This decision is taken by national government officials in consultation with their national ministry of defense. The senior national government representative and the national TF commander will determine the direction of military activities on the ground.

g. Although it is the primary responsibility of national civilian aid agencies, governmental departments and agencies, civil facility authorities, and international agencies to conduct disaster needs assessments, they may not have the ability to do so or capability to respond fast enough depending on the complexity, size, and nature of the emergency/crisis. In such cases, along with multilateral and bilateral agreements, military forces may be requested to provide and/or assist in disaster needs assessments.

For NATO-specific doctrine, see AJP-3.4, Allied Joint Doctrine for Non-Article 5 Crisis Response Operations.

APPENDIX A
PLANNING CONSIDERATIONS

Multinational operations as described in this publication cover a wide spectrum of subjects. The checklist below provides an MNFC with a planning tool for multinational operations directed through either an integrated or LN scenario. Operations conducted in a parallel command relationship will normally follow national planning guidance and doctrine. **Where possible, this checklist will attempt to highlight *only* those items *unique* to multinational operations.**

Detailed planning checklists for JTF directorates can be found in JP 3-33, Joint Task Force Headquarters. *Most material contained in those checklists is applicable to MNTF directorates as well.*

Strategic-Level Considerations

_____ Has the political-military estimate been completed and coordinated with national-level partner nations? Have the partner nations reached agreement on the appropriate response?

_____ Have strategic assessments been shared within the constraints of national and organizational information sharing regulations?

_____ Has the LN, in coordination with other partner nations, developed the strategic military guidance for the operation? Does this strategic guidance contain:

    _____ A clear description of political objectives?

    _____ A broad outline of any military activity envisioned?

    _____ The desired end state?

    _____ Key planning assumptions?

    _____ Constraints or restraints on military operations and actions?

_____ Has a mission analysis been accomplished?

    _____ Has the commander's mission statement been provided?

    _____ Has an analysis of the situation, opposition forces, friendly forces, and restrictions been conducted?

_____ Have COAs been developed?

    _____ Has a preferred COA been selected?

    _____ Has the commander's intent been developed/provided?

_____ Have ROE been agreed upon by military commanders and national policy makers?

_____ Has a CONOPS been developed and approved by the national and interagency partners?

_____ Has a confirmation of capabilities and/or forces to be contributed been obtained from our national and interagency partners, to include government capabilities/forces and likely IGO, NGO, and/or private sector contributors?

_____ Has an OPLAN been developed based on the approved CONOPS?

_____ Have annexes to OPLANs/CONPLANs been developed to effectively support multinational and/or interagency coordination and operations?

_____ Has the OPLAN been approved by national and interagency partners?

_____ Has the operational-level commander been appointed?

_____ Has communication synchronization guidance been included in the OPLAN?

_____ Has the appropriate coordination been conducted with the DOS Bureau of Conflict and Stabilization Operations, their associated local humanitarian reconstruction and stabilization teams, United States Agency for International Development, and/or the US embassy country team(s) in the specific OA?

_____ Has IO guidance been included in every phase of the OPLAN?

Operational-Level Considerations

_____ Have command relationships been established between the MNFC and national forces?

_____ Has an MNTF HQ been established?

_____ Have critical billet requirements been identified?

_____ Has a theater foreign disclosure authority been identified? Has a policy and a plan for the control, release, and dissemination of sensitive information been promulgated?

_____ Have the personnel for the multinational staff been chosen to reflect the required functional skills, training levels, and language? Have historical national sensitivities been considered?

_____ Are there sufficient linguists available for both planning and execution?

_____ Do liaison elements have appropriate linguistic, communications, logistic, and office support capabilities in place?

_____ Has the command structure been designed to minimize layers to a more horizontal organization?

_____ Have 24-hour command centers been established if required?

_____ Have C2 arrangements been made to include appropriate IGO and NGO officials in coordinating functions?

_____ Have multinational legal constraints been considered in planning for C2?

_____ Have the multinational partners with a lesser C2 capability been provided appropriate liaison personnel and interpreters (if necessary), operators, and maintainers to enable interaction with the commander and other multinational members?

_____ Have arrangements been made for intra- and inter-staff communication among same nation staff members?

_____ Have the strategic and military end states been identified? Are the conditions tangible in military terms? Are they contained in the mission statement?

_____ Has the end state and exit strategy been articulated as part of the commander's vision for subordinates?

_____ What is the exit strategy?

_____ What constitutes mission success?

_____ Has a mission analysis been conducted?

_____ Has planning guidance been developed and issued?

_____ Does it contain the commander's intent?

_____ Are the ROE established? Do they require adjustment?

_____ Have COAs been developed?

_____ Has a preferred COA been selected?

_____ Has the commander's intent been provided/developed?

_____ Has the deployment time-phased force and deployment data (TPFDD) been completed and validated?

_____ Have the non-US forces relying on strategic mobility for deployment and/or redeployment been included in the TPFDD?

_____ Has the deployment plan been deconflicted with HN, NGO, and contractor transportation requirements in order to avoid competition for limited transportation infrastructure?

_____ Has the probable cost of the multinational operations been determined and are there mechanisms in place to track the cost?

_____ Have logisticians assessed the feasibility and/or supportability and risks of the mission?

_____ Is the MNFC aware of existing agreements among participating nations in the form of bilateral or multilateral arrangements, funding, and training?

_____ Have SOFAs been agreed to? If not, who should conduct negotiations? Who has been designated to negotiate technical agreements to implement SOFAs?

_____ Do the resources allocated to the force protection component of the mission balance with the potential political ramifications of failure to protect the force?

_____ Have the cultural, social, political, and economic dynamics of the OA been fused with the traditional study of geographic and military considerations to form an intelligence estimate that identifies threat centers of gravity, as well as high-value and high-payoff targets? Does the plan consider these issues in a way that facilitates operations and end state?

_____ Have determined efforts been made to pool information with applicable NGOs, to increase efficiency of operations through coordination and eliminate redundancy in operations?

_____ Are nonlethal weapons available for use?

_____ To what extent are riot control agents authorized for use?

_____ To what extent are nonlethal weapons authorized for use?

_____ Are forces, communication system capabilities, and logistic support robust enough to respond to increased levels of operational intensity?

_____ Has coordination been accomplished with multinational members regarding communication equipment capability?

_____ Has coordination been accomplished regarding frequency assignment?

_____ Has the terrain and environment been considered while planning for the communication system network?

_____ Have common databases been provided for?

_____ Has the nation most capable of providing an integrated, interoperable communication system network been selected to serve as network manager for the multinational communication system infrastructure?

_____ Have agreements on cryptographic, communications and/or ADP security issues, and other planning factors been reached among all multinational components? Are compatible materials available?

_____ Have arrangements been made and/or established to allow contract multinational foreign nation employees to work on C2 staffs without exposure to ADP and classified information used in daily operations?

_____ Have the nations agreed to work on a standard datum and produce all products to that datum?

_____ Has a multinational geospatial intelligence plan been produced and disseminated which designates all products for use?

_____ Have special, adequate, and supportable intelligence sharing and foreign disclosure procedures been established?

_____ Have special, adequate, and supportable geospatial sharing and foreign disclosure procedures been established?

_____ Have special, adequate, and supportable biometrics sharing and foreign disclosure procedures been established?

_____ Have the intelligence requirements been clearly stated to focus the collection effort?

_____ Has the adversary's use of space assets been analyzed and have requests for denying militarily useful space information to the adversary been considered?

_____ Have efforts been made to place sufficient intelligence collection resources under the control of (or at least immediately responsive to) the MNFC?

_____ Have efforts been made to assign intelligence gathering tasks IAW the MNFC's intelligence requirements and according to the capability of the multinational equipment under MNF control?

_____ Have efforts been made to pool intelligence and battlefield information into multinational centralized processing and exploitation centers? Have disclosure and release procedures been identified, with respect to each partner nation?

_____ Can authorized targeting materials be disseminated rapidly?

_____ Has the MNFC's authority to redistribute logistic assets and services been defined and agreed to?

_____ What, if any, ACSAs exist between participating nations to enable the provision of supplies, services, transportation, and logistic support?

_____ Does principal logistics civil augmentation program structure have an overall officer in charge or main point of contact for C2 of contract personnel?

_____ Do other legal authorities permit the provision of logistic support to participating nations?

_____ Have reimbursement or replacement-in-kind procedures been developed and agreed to?

_____ Have contractor procedures been established?

_____ Is there a means in place which authorizes exchange of mutual logistic support of goods and services between the MNTF countries and accounts for the amounts received?

_____ Has a logistics determination been made (i.e., what countries will provide what piece of the logistics system, health services to include ground and air evacuation, and health service logistics)?

_____ Have logistic reporting procedures been established and promulgated throughout the force?

_____ Can the HN provide support, and if so, have negotiations to secure support been established or completed?

_____ Are the mission economic and infrastructure repair plans known and being complied with by all nations, Services, and units?

_____ Has HNS been evaluated in the deployed location(s) to determine the logistic requirements?

_____ Has an assessment of HN medical capabilities and a determination of availability to support MNF health services requirements been accomplished?

_____ Have coordinating centers been established for personnel movement, medical support, ground and air evacuation, operational contract support, infrastructure engineering, and logistic operations?

_____ Is a transitional plan available to facilitate deployment and operational assumption of in-place contracts, equipment, facilities, and personnel belonging to another agency or alliance?

_____ Has funding been identified to support operations and/or to provide reimbursement of expenditures from existing budgets?

     _____ Will common funding be available to support multinational common costs and expenditures?

     _____ Has it been determined if or to what extent operational-related expenses will be reimbursed from common funding or sources external to national funding by the participating nations?

_____ Are medical facilities identified to support the operation? Are evacuation plans, both intra- and inter-theater, in place?

     _____ Are CBRN threats known, and are troops and medical facilities prepared to cope with their possible use?

_____ Are graves registration and mortuary procedures in place to service multinational casualties, to include recognition of cultural differences in dealing with casualties?

_____ Have IO activities been planned to support the operation?

     _____ Have assets been requested to support the IO plan?

     _____ Have procedures been established for coordination and approval of IO activities?

     _____ Have military information support personnel been integrated into analysis, targeting, and planning?

_____ Have IO capabilities been integrated and tailored to the specific environment/mission assigned?

_____ Have population and resource control measures and the subordinate commander's authority to impose them been included in the MNF plan?

_____ Are there adequate CA personnel on hand to assist planners?

_____ Are there special operations personnel available to develop and execute unconventional military options for the commander?

_____ Has a PA plan been promulgated that:

     _____ Provides a contingency statement to use in response to media queries before initial public release of information concerning the MNF and its mission?

_____ States who (from which nation and when, or all nations simultaneously) makes the initial public release concerning the MNF and its mission?

_____ States agreed-upon procedures for the subsequent release of information concerning the MNF and its national components?

_____ Is predeployment media training complete?

_____ Is the relationship between the inevitable media coverage of tactical operations and future strategic decisions understood by all commanders?

_____ Have requirements for combat camera support been arranged?

_____ Has an operation historian been designated and staff authorized?

_____ Is a mechanism in place for the collection, assessment, and reporting of lessons learned?

_____ Who will determine when the transition begins or is complete?

_____ What are the redeployment and/or withdrawal plans for MNFs? Is the departure of forces to be accomplished under tactical conditions?

_____ What are the environmental standards to be met by withdrawal in humanitarian or other peaceful operations?

_____ What forces, equipment, and supplies will remain behind? Has disposal of equipment and supplies been properly planned?

_____ What are the C2 and command arrangements for departure?

_____ Who will support forces that remain behind?

_____ Has the C2 systems support required for the diminishing MNF presence been identified?

APPENDIX B
MULTINATIONAL PLANNING AUGMENTATION TEAM

1. Overview

a. The MPAT program was established by the Commander, US Pacific Command (USPACOM), in consultation with the chiefs of defense of various nations in the Asia-Pacific region in early 2000. The impetus for the program is to facilitate the rapid and effective establishment and/or augmentation of MNTF HQ.

b. MPAT is not a program with formal participatory agreements. The key factor in program success to date has been the informal ad hoc nature of the program. Without MOAs, terms of reference, or other more formal arrangements, the program has been able to share information, and all participants have been able to jointly develop concepts and procedures without the normal formal policy constraints—a key inhibitor to multinational interoperability when working with other nations.

2. Multinational Planning Augmentation Team Composition

a. MPAT is an international cadre of military planners from 31 nations with interests in the Asia-Pacific region that is capable of augmenting an MNF HQ established to plan and execute coalition operations in response to military engagement, SC, and deterrence operations and small-scale contingencies. Planners learn from each other the common procedures for activating, forming, and employing a coalition TF HQ and associated planning processes. This is done through a series of multinational workshops called MPAT TEMPEST EXPRESS staff planning workshops. The MPAT cadre also participates in USPACOM and other nations' multinational exercises.

b. Participation also includes representation from UN organizations, IGOs, and NGOs.

c. The MPAT Secretariat resides with the Pacific Command Exercises Directorate.

3. Multinational Force Standing Operating Procedures

a. MPAT planners are credited with developing an SOP for an MNTF HQ. This SOP recognizes the existence of shared national interests in the region and seeks to standardize some basic concepts and processes that will promote habits of cooperation, increase dialogue, and provide for baseline MNTF operational concepts. Further, this SOP serves as a centerpiece for the MPAT workshops and exercises aimed at improving interoperability and MNTF operational readiness within the Asia-Pacific region. The purpose of the SOP is straightforward:

(1) Increase the speed of an MNF initial response.

(2) Improve interoperability among the participating forces.

(3) Enhance overall mission effectiveness.

(4) Support unity of effort.

b. The MNF SOP is not a USPACOM document, nor is it signed by any of the participants. It has been developed by the combined efforts of all the MPAT nations as a multinational document to provide the foundation of multinational crisis response. The SOP is also unclassified and available for use by any nation in combined or coalition operations.

c. The procedures contained in the MNF SOP are primarily focused for use by an MNTF HQ for use at the mid to lower end of the range of military operations. These include numerous missions such as combat operations in small-scale contingencies, stability operations, PO (which includes peace building, peacekeeping, peace enforcement, and peacemaking), FHA, military assisted NEO, SAR/PR, combating terrorism, and FID.

4. Organization

The MPAT is not a standing, billeted organization or TF. It is a cadre or pool of trained planners with MNF operations planning expertise that has developed relationships from participation in MPAT events. Figure B-1 contains a list of potential key MNTF staff billets or functional areas that can be filled with MPAT personnel from the various MNF participating nations.

For additional information on the MPAT concept and MNF SOP, refer to the unclassified MPAT Web site. URL: https://community.apan.org/mpat or www.mpat.org. This Web site acts as the portal for the MPAT program and MNF SOP. The updated MNF SOP can be obtained via this portal and the latest MPAT information can be found through this site.

Multinational Planning Augmentation Team Augmentation Roles

- Civil-military
- Medical
- Legal
- Public affairs
- Military information support operations
- Operational planners
- Personnel
- Intelligence
- Logistics
- Communications
- Engineering
- Force movement and deployment

- Force protection
- Ground operations
- Maritime operations
- Air operations
- Special operations
- Marine operations
- Sealift
- Airlift
- Information operations
- Air logistics
- Network/collaboration
- Space operations

Figure B-1. Multinational Planning Augmentation Team Augmentation Roles

---

APPENDIX C
MULTINATIONAL INTEROPERABILITY COUNCIL

1. Overview

a. The MIC is a joint, multinational forum for identifying interoperability issues and articulating actions at the strategic and high operational level that, if nationally implemented by MIC member nations, will contribute to more effective coalition operations.

b. The MIC is a senior operator led body for coordinating, deliberating, and facilitating resolution of interoperability issues. The MIC's work focuses on resolving information interoperability problems, strategic and operational issues, and interagency aspects considered as key to coalition operations.

c. While the MIC's initial work was focused on resolving information interoperability challenges, the scope of the MIC has expanded significantly to cover other strategic and operational issues considered to be key to identifying and articulating interoperability issues and deficiencies impacting multinational operations. The MIC focuses on resolving information sharing, operational, and LN interoperability issues across all lines of development (doctrine, organization, training, material, leadership, personnel, and facilities). The MIC also addresses interagency/comprehensive approach activities that are key in establishing and executing coalitions, as well as policy issues for supporting and monitoring multinational operations. These activities are targeted to positively impact coalition interoperability policy, doctrine, and collaborative planning and execution.

2. Composition

a. The MIC is a seven-nation forum composed of countries that are most likely to form and lead a coalition operation. The MIC member nations are Australia, Canada, France, Germany, Italy, the United Kingdom, and the US. The member nations are equal participants in the MIC. While membership is not meant to be exclusionary, the criteria for membership is based upon a nation's demonstrated capacity and national will to lead international coalitions.

b. The MIC is led by the MIC Principals, who are the senior national representatives for MIC member nations and are flag officers/general officers from their nation's national defense HQ. The MIC Principals are responsible for defining and articulating the strategic direction of the MIC and for providing guidance for the MIC activities. Invaluable levels of trust and camaraderie are cultivated in the MIC, which further encourage and promote national efforts in coalition and multinational operations.

c. The following groups manage and/or implement/perform the work of the MIC according to the guidance of the MIC Principals:

(1) The steering group (SG) is composed of O-6/NATO OF-5 representatives and is responsible for providing management oversight of tasks approved by the MIC Principals. It is the senior O-6/NATO OF-5-level group responsible for providing day-to-day guidance,

oversight, and direction to the standing and directed multinational interoperability working groups (MIWGs).

(2) The MIC consists of two standing MIWGs with different scopes; the operations and the operations support working group. The operations MIWG focuses on issues associated with current and future coalition operations from a cross-functional perspective. The operations support MIWG is task oriented and focused on operational enablers in support of coalition operations. Directed MIWGs are stood up on the direction of the principals to address a specific or a group of specific tasks. A directed MIWG is time limited with an expected duration of 12 months; continuation will be reviewed annually. Each MIC nation provides at least one representative (O-6/O-5 - NATO OF-5/OF-4) to each of the MIWGs. Through analysis of national positions with respect to concepts, policy, experimentation, lessons learned, doctrine, and other relevant areas, the MIWG's aim is to inform and support coalition building and operations and influence the development of operational practices to enable more effective coalition operations.

(3) The MIC Executive Secretariat (ES) staff is the only full-time MIC staff and works in the US Joint Staff Operations Directorate in the Pentagon. The MIC ES staff is responsible for managing and coordinating the day-to-day business activities for the MIC while serving as the central point of contact for the MIC Principals, the SG, and the functional MIWGs. In addition to permanently assigned US personnel, two non-US officers from other MIC member nations are assigned full time to the MIC ES staff. The MIC ES staff conducts all external coordination, correspondence, and communication with the staffs of non-MIC nations and organizations as well as other combined multinational organizations on matters of mutual interest to the MIC: ABCA Standardization Program, ASIC, AUSCANNZUKUS, CCEB, NATO, Quadrilateral Logistics Forum, and the Technical Cooperation Program.

d. Other nations and organizations can participate in MIC activities as affiliates or observers to address common interoperability issues. Affiliates have an enduring, ongoing relationship with the MIC. Observers are nations/organizations that attend MIC meetings on a one-time or short-term basis to support a specific event or activity that addresses interoperability challenges or leverages ongoing MIC activities. Currently New Zealand, NATO Allied Command Transformation, and the Military Staff of the EU are MIC affiliates.

3. Accomplishments

MIC-developed documents represent a nonbinding consensus view among MIC nations. These documents are reviewed and updated on a regular basis. The following are representative examples of MIC-developed documents. Refer to the MIC community on the All Partners Access Network (APAN) Web site for the most current version of all MIC documents.

a. **Coalition Building Guide (CBG)**

(1) One of the MIC's early actions was the development of the CBG. The purpose of the CBG is to facilitate LNs, troop contributing nations, and participants in the

establishment and effective operation of a coalition anywhere on the globe. Specifically, the CBG concentrates on the strategic and operational levels of multinational joint operations and identifies some of the essential factors associated with the process of coalition building. Additionally, it attempts to provide a common framework of reference for contributing nations. The CBG is designed to assist the JFC and his staff as well as highlight national factors. The CBG does not constitute official policy or doctrine, nor does it represent a definitive staff planning or military decision-making guide. It is offered to assist MIC member nations and their potential partners in serving together in future coalitions, and to assist other MIWGs in their exploration of related interoperability issues. The CBG is based upon the LN concept. For the purposes of the CBG, the LN is described as:

The LN is that nation with the will and capability, competence, and influence to provide the essential elements of political consultation and military leadership to coordinate the planning, mounting, and execution of a coalition military operation. Within the overarching organizational framework provided by the LN, other nations participating in the coalition may be designated as functional lead agent(s) to provide and/or coordinate specific critical sub-functions of the operation and its execution, based on national capability. These constructs may apply at the strategic, operational, and/or tactical levels.

(2) The MIC agreed that NATO Allied joint doctrine, unless otherwise specifically directed, is default doctrine for planning and conducting multinational operations. The CBG uses established NATO Allied joint doctrine as a basis. NATO doctrine is the default doctrine for a MIC-led coalition unless the LN specifies the military doctrine to be used. If an LN chooses to use other than NATO doctrine, then it must ensure all participating partners have access to the doctrine in use. Operating procedures as well as TTP will be prescribed by the LN.

For additional guidance on the CBG, refer to the Multinational Interoperability Council Coalition Building Guide, *3rd edition, Version 1, 7 November 2012.*

b. **Comprehensive Approach Framework—A Military Perspective**

(1) Recent experiences of coalition operations in Afghanistan, Iraq, Kosovo, and other operations confirm the complexity of contemporary crises. Complex crises do not lend themselves to simple definition or analysis. Today's challenges demand a comprehensive approach by the international community, including the coordinated action from an appropriate range of civil and military actors, enabled by the orchestration, coordination, and deconfliction of coalitions' military and political instruments with the other instruments of power.

(2) The comprehensive approach framework is primarily designed for use by prospective coalition commanders and their staffs, but it also informs potential civilian partners on the vision and views of the militaries organized within the MIC concerning the framework for the application of a comprehensive approach as both a mindset and a method to crisis prevention, crisis management, and post-conflict activities. The central idea is to demonstrate the possibilities but also the limitations of forming civil-military partnerships both at home and in a region or a country in need of an international engagement by creating

and operationalizing the spirit of a true team effort. The document therefore aims at establishing a certain commonality in comprehensive approach understanding and terminology in order to support further work between military and civilian partners in the context of coalition operations.

(3) In order to promote the synergies of a civil-military team effort, the national militaries of the MIC nations have to specify their roles and possible contributions throughout all phases of involvement in a crisis abroad. These phases of conflict have been categorized as crisis prevention, stabilization, and finally transition—when the military involvement winds down in order to be handed over to other, better suited actors. This expeditionary focus excludes all questions of how the individual MIC nations handle natural or man-made crises within their own respective boundaries, possibly also in a comprehensive manner. Likewise, possible considerations for a civil-military interface in situations of high-intensity warfare are not subject to the framework at hand.

(4) The document points out the products and services needed from civilian partners, which may range from an early exchange of cultural views to very precise demands for specific liaison arrangements. Acknowledging the existing overlap with civilian organizations and actors, the areas of military logistics and military medical services have been given special attention.

(5) The underlying core theme throughout the document applies the following triple concept in order to make the envisaged civil-military team effort a reality:

(a) Establishing a common understanding of the problem at hand (which includes information sharing and SA),

(b) Defining a mutually acceptable vision for the problem solution (which includes a set of outcomes or objectives that shall not contradict one another), and

(c) Aiming at harmonizing the corresponding activities (which includes the will to adjust in light of emerging insights).

c. **The Military Contribution to Stabilization Operations (Stabilization Handbook)**

(1) Stabilization is a multidimensional concept involving reconstruction and normalization activities and tasks that involves attributes of other programs such as disarmament, demobilization, and reintegration and security sector reform (SSR) that must be considered in defining common approaches to a campaign.

(2) The *Stabilization Handbook* addresses the tasks normally performed by military forces in supporting stabilization operations when an HN is unable to govern and/or to provide for the basic needs of its citizens. Military forces perform myriad functions in supporting broad coalition reconstruction, SSR, and stabilization efforts in order to establish a safe and secure environment in a fragile state. The stabilization tasks accomplished by military forces during a wide range of activities help set the conditions or framework for:

(a) Facilitating reconciliation among local or regional adversaries;

(b) Establishing political, legal, social, and economic institutions; and

(c) Setting the environment for transitioning responsibility to legitimate civil authority operating under the rule of law.

(3) Accordingly, the document also addresses the need to consider a comprehensive approach in planning for and conducting stabilization operations, in order to build strong relationships through cooperation, collaboration, and coordination with the various governmental, nongovernmental, private, and international organizations and agencies, as well as other military forces involved in stabilization operations.

For additional information on the MIC and ongoing multinational interoperability efforts, refer to the MIC community on the APAN Web site, https://community.apan.org/mic.

Intentionally Blank

APPENDIX D
REFERENCES

The development of JP 3-16 is based upon the following primary references.

1. Executive Branch Documents

a. Presidential Policy Directive-1, *Organization of the National Security Council System.*

b. NSPD-44, *Management of Interagency Efforts Concerning Reconstruction and Stabilization.*

c. NDP-1, *National Policy and Procedures for the Disclosure of Classified Military Information to Foreign Governments and International Organizations.*

d. National Security Decision Memorandum 119, *Disclosure of Classified United States Military Information to Foreign Governments and International Organizations.*

e. Director of Central Intelligence Directive 6/7, *National Disclosure Policy.*

f. *National Strategy for Information Sharing.*

g. Intelligence Community Directive Number 710, *Classification and Control Markings System.*

2. Department of Defense Documents

a. DOD Information Sharing Strategy.

b. DOD Manual 5200.01, Volume 1, *DOD Information Security Program: Overview, Classification, and Declassification.*

c. DOD Manual 5200.01, Volume 3, *DOD Information Security Program: Protection of Classified Information.*

d. DOD 7000.14R, *Department of Defense Financial Management Regulation (DODFMR).*

e. DODD 2010.9, *Acquisition and Cross-Servicing Agreements.*

f. DODD 2310.01E, *The Department of Defense Detainee Program.*

g. DODD 2311.01E, *DOD Law of War Program.*

h. DODD 5100.01, *Functions of the Department of Defense and Its Major Components.*

i. DODD 5101.1, *DOD Executive Agent.*

j. Defense Security Cooperation Agency Manual 5105.38-M, *Security Assistance Management Manual.*

k. DODD 5132.03, *Department of Defense Policy and Responsibilities Relating to Security Cooperation.*

l. DODD 5205.02E *DOD Operations Security (OPSEC) Program.*

m. DODD 5230.11, *Disclosure of Classified Military Information to Foreign Governments and International Organizations.*

n. DODD 5530.3, *International Agreements.*

o. DODI 3000.05, *Stability Operations.*

p. DODI 5000.68, *Security Force Assistance.*

q. DODI 8110.1, *Multinational Information Sharing Networks Implementation.*

r. DODI 8523.01, *Communications Security (COMSEC).*

3. Chairman of the Joint Chiefs of Staff Publications

a. CJCSI 2120.01B, *Acquisition and Cross-Servicing Agreements.*

b. CJCSI 2700.01E, *International Military Agreements for Rationalization, Standardization, and Interoperability (RSI) Between the United States, Its Allies and Other Friendly Nations.*

c. CJCSI 3121.01B, *Standing Rules of Engagement/Standing Rules for the Use of Force for US Forces.*

d. CJCSI 5120.02C, *Joint Doctrine Development System.*

e. CJCSI 5221.01C, *Delegation of Authority to Commanders of Combatant Commands to Disclose Classified Military Information to Foreign Governments and International Organizations.*

f. CJCSI 5715.01C, *Joint Staff Participation in Interagency Affairs.*

g. CJCSI 5810.01D, *Implementation of the DOD Law of War Program.*

h. CJCSI 6510.01F, *Information Assurance (IA) and Support to Computer Network Defense (CND).*

i. CJCSI 6510.06B, *Communication Security Releases to Foreign Nations.*

j. CJCSI 6610.01D, *Tactical Data Link Standardization Implementation Plan.*

k. CJCSI 6711.01B, *Exchange of Communications.*

l. CJCSI 6740.01B, *Military Telecommunications Agreements and Arrangements Between the United States and Regional Defense Organizations or Friendly Foreign Nations.*

m. Chairman of the Joint Chiefs of Staff Manual (CJCSM) 5120.01, *Joint Doctrine Development Process.*

n. CJCSM 6120.01E, *Joint Multi-Tactical Data Link Operating Procedures.*

o. JP 1, *Doctrine for the Armed Forces of the United States.*

p. JP 1-0, *Joint Personnel Support.*

q. JP 1-02, *Department of Defense Dictionary of Military and Associated Terms.*

r. JP 2-0, *Joint Intelligence.*

s. JP 2-01, *Joint and National Intelligence Support to Military Operations.*

t. JP 2-03, *Geospatial Intelligence Support to Joint Operations.*

u. JP 3-0, *Joint Operations.*

v. JP 3-01, *Countering Air and Missile Threats.*

w. JP 3-03, *Joint Interdiction.*

x. JP 3-05, *Special Operations.*

y. JP 3-07, *Stability Operations.*

z. JP 3-07.3, *Peace Operations.*

aa. JP 3-07.4, *Joint Counterdrug Operations.*

bb. JP 3-08, *Interorganizational Coordination During Joint Operations.*

cc. JP 3-09, *Joint Fire Support.*

dd. JP 3-11, *Operations in Chemical, Biological, Radiological, and Nuclear (CBRN) Environments.*

ee. JP 3-13, *Information Operations.*

ff. JP 3-13.2, *Military Information Support Operations.*

gg. JP 3-14, *Space Operations.*

hh. JP 3-18, *Joint Forcible Entry Operations*.

ii. JP 3-22, *Foreign Internal Defense*.

jj. JP 3-24, *Counterinsurgency Operations*.

kk. JP 3-26, *Counterterrorism*.

ll. JP 3-27, *Homeland Defense*.

mm. JP 3-28, *Defense Support of Civil Authorities*.

nn. JP 3-29, *Foreign Humanitarian Assistance*.

oo. JP 3-30, *Command and Control for Joint Air Operations*.

pp. JP 3-31, *Command and Control for Joint Land Operations*.

qq. JP 3-32, *Command and Control of Joint Maritime Operations*.

rr. JP 3-33, *Joint Task Force Headquarters*.

ss. JP 3-34, *Joint Engineer Operations*.

tt. JP 3-50, *Personnel Recovery*.

uu. JP 3-52, *Joint Airspace Control*.

vv. JP 3-57, *Civil-Military Operations*.

ww. JP 3-59, *Meteorological and Oceanographic Operations*.

xx. JP 3-61, *Public Affairs*.

yy. JP 3-63, *Detainee Operations*.

zz. JP 3-68, *Noncombatant Evacuation Operations*.

aaa. JP 4-0, *Joint Logistics*.

bbb. JP 4-02, *Health Services*.

ccc. JP 4-08, *Logistics in Support of Multinational Operations*.

ddd. JP 4-09, *Distribution Operations*.

eee. JP 5-0, *Joint Operation Planning*.

fff. JP 6-0, *Joint Communications System*.

ggg. JP 6-01, *Joint Electromagnetic Spectrum Management Operations.*

hhh. *Guidance for Employment of the Force (GEF).*

iii. *Joint Strategic Capabilities Plan (JSCP).*

4. Allied Joint Publications

a. AJP-3.3.5, *Airspace Control.*

b. AJP-3.4, *Allied Joint Doctrine for Non Article 5 Crisis Response Operations.*

c. AJP-3.4.2, *Allied Joint Doctrine for Non-Combatant Evacuation Operations.*

d. AJP-6, *Allied Joint Doctrine for Communications and Information Systems.*

e. AJP-9, *Allied Joint Doctrine for Civil-Military Cooperation.*

5. Other Publications

a. Army Tactics, Techniques, and Procedures 3-92.3, *Digital Liaison Detachments.*

b. Multinational Planning Augmentation Team (MPAT) Concept and Supporting information, www.mpat.org or https://community.apan.org/mpat.

c. Multinational Planning Augmentation Team (MPAT), *Multinational Force Standing Operating Procedures (MNF-SOP)*, Version 2.8, August 2012. https://community.apan.org/mpat.

d. MIC, *Coalition Building Guide*, 3rd edition, Version 1, 7 November 2012.

e. National Strategy for Information Sharing.

Intentionally Blank

APPENDIX E
ADMINISTRATIVE INSTRUCTIONS

1. User Comments

Users in the field are highly encouraged to submit comments on this publication to: Joint Staff J-7, Deputy Director, Joint Education and Doctrine, ATTN: Joint Doctrine Analysis Division, 116 Lake View Parkway, Suffolk, VA 23435-2697. These comments should address content (accuracy, usefulness, consistency, and organization), writing, and appearance.

2. Authorship

The lead agent and Joint Staff doctrine sponsor for this publication is the Director for Operations (J-3).

3. Supersession

This publication supersedes JP 3-16, 7 March 2007, *Multinational Operations*.

4. Change Recommendations

a. Recommendations for urgent changes to this publication should be submitted:

TO: JOINT STAFF WASHINGTON DC//J3//

INFO: JOINT STAFF WASHINGTON DC//J7-JE&D//

b. Routine changes should be submitted electronically to the Deputy Director, Joint Education and Doctrine, ATTN: Joint Doctrine Analysis Division, 116 Lake View Parkway, Suffolk, VA 23435-2697, and info the lead agent and the Director for Joint Force Development, J-7/JE&D.

c. When a Joint Staff directorate submits a proposal to the CJCS that would change source document information reflected in this publication, that directorate will include a proposed change to this publication as an enclosure to its proposal. The Services and other organizations are requested to notify the Joint Staff J-7 when changes to source documents reflected in this publication are initiated.

5. Distribution of Publications

Local reproduction is authorized, and access to unclassified publications is unrestricted. However, access to and reproduction authorization for classified JPs must be IAW DOD Manual 5200.01, Volume 1, *DOD Information Security Program: Overview, Classification, and Declassification,* and DOD Manual 5200.01, Volume 3, *DOD Information Security Program: Protection of Classified Information.*

6. Distribution of Electronic Publications

a. Joint Staff J-7 will not print copies of JPs for distribution. Electronic versions are available on JDEIS at https://jdeis.js.mil (NIPRNET) and http://jdeis.js.smil.mil (SIPRNET), and on the JEL at http://www.dtic.mil/doctrine (NIPRNET).

b. Only approved JPs and joint test publications are releasable outside the CCMDs, Services, and Joint Staff. Release of any classified JP to foreign governments or foreign nationals must be requested through the local embassy (Defense Attaché Office) to DIA, Defense Foreign Liaison/IE-3, 200 MacDill Blvd., Joint Base Anacostia-Bolling, Washington, DC 20340-5100.

c. JEL CD-ROM. Upon request of a joint doctrine development community member, the Joint Staff J-7 will produce and deliver one CD-ROM with current JPs. This JEL CD-ROM will be updated not less than semi-annually and when received can be locally reproduced for use within the CCMDs, Services, and combat support agencies.

GLOSSARY
PART I—ABBREVIATIONS AND ACRONYMS

AADC	area air defense commander
ABCA	American, British, Canadian, Australian and New Zealand
ACA	airspace control authority
ACSA	acquisition and cross-servicing agreement
ADP	automated data processing
AJP	allied joint publication
AO	area of operations
AP	allied publication
APAN	All Partners Access Network
ASIC	Air and Space Interoperability Council
AUSCANNZUKUS	Australian, Canadian, New Zealand, United Kingdom, United States
C2	command and control
CA	civil affairs
CBG	coalition building guide
CBRN	chemical, biological, radiological, and nuclear
CCC	coalition coordination center
CCDR	combatant commander
CCEB	Combined Communications-Electronics Board
CCMD	combatant command
CD	counterdrug
CID	combat identification
CIMIC	civil-military cooperation
CJCS	Chairman of the Joint Chiefs of Staff
CJCSI	Chairman of the Joint Chiefs of Staff instruction
CJCSM	Chairman of the Joint Chiefs of Staff manual
CMO	civil-military operations
CMOC	civil-military operations center
COA	course of action
COMSEC	communications security
CONOPS	concept of operations
CONPLAN	concept plan
DIDO	designated intelligence disclosure official
DLD	digital liaison detachment
DOD	Department of Defense
DODD	Department of Defense directive
DODI	Department of Defense instruction
DOS	Department of State
DSPD	defense support to public diplomacy

ES	executive secretariat
EU	European Union
FDO	foreign disclosure officer
FHA	foreign humanitarian assistance
FHP	force health protection
FID	foreign internal defense
FSF	foreign security forces
GCC	geographic combatant commander
GEF	Guidance for Employment of the Force
HN	host nation
HNS	host-nation support
HNSCC	host-nation support coordination cell
HQ	headquarters
IAW	in accordance with
IGO	intergovernmental organization
IHC	international humanitarian community
IO	information operations
IRC	information-related capability
ISA	international standardization agreement
ISAF	International Security Assistance Force
J-2	intelligence directorate of a joint staff
JFC	joint force commander
JP	joint publication
JSCP	Joint Strategic Capabilities Plan
JTF	joint task force
LNO	liaison officer
LOAC	law of armed conflict
LOC	line of communications
MCI	multinational communications integration
METOC	meteorological and oceanographic
MIC	Multinational Interoperability Council
MISO	military information support operations
MIWG	multinational interoperability working group
MNCC	multinational coordination center
MNF	multinational force
MNFACC	multinational force air component commander
MNFC	multinational force commander
MNFLCC	multinational force land component commander

MNFMCC	multinational force maritime component commander
MNFSOCC	multinational force special operations component commander
MNTF	multinational task force
MOA	memorandum of agreement
MOU	memorandum of understanding
MP	multinational publication
MPAT	Multinational Planning Augmentation Team
NATO	North Atlantic Treaty Organization
NDP	national disclosure policy
NEO	noncombatant evacuation operation
NGO	nongovernmental organization
NSPD	national security Presidential directive
OA	operational area
OE	operational environment
OPCON	operational control
OPLAN	operation plan
OPSEC	operations security
PA	public affairs
PM	patient movement
PO	peace operations
PR	personnel recovery
PRCC	personnel recovery coordination center
ROE	rules of engagement
RSI	rationalization, standardization, and interoperability
SA	situational awareness
SAR	search and rescue
SC	security cooperation
SCA	space coordinating authority
SecDef	Secretary of Defense
SFA	security force assistance
SG	steering group
SIPRNET	SECRET Internet Protocol Router Network
SJA	staff judge advocate
SOF	special operations forces
SOFA	status-of-forces agreement
SOP	standing operating procedure
SPP	State Partnership Program
SSR	security sector reform
STANAG	standardization agreement (NATO)

TA   technical arrangement
TACON   tactical control
TCP   theater campaign plan
TF   task force
TPFDD   time-phased force and deployment data
TTP   tactics, techniques, and procedures

UN   United Nations
USG   United States Government
USPACOM   United States Pacific Command
USSTRATCOM   United States Strategic Command

civil affairs agreement. None. (Approved for removal from JP 1-02.)

combined. A term identifying two or more forces or agencies of two or more allies operating together. (Approved for incorporation into JP 1-02.)

combined force. None. (Approved for removal from JP 1-02.)

common supplies. None. (Approved for removal from JP 1-02.)

integrated staff. A staff in which one officer only is appointed to each post on the establishment of the headquarters, irrespective of nationality and Service. (Approved for incorporation into JP 1-02 with JP 3-16 as the source JP.)

lead nation. The nation with the will, capability, competence, and influence to provide the essential elements of political consultation and military leadership to coordinate the planning, mounting, and execution of a multinational operation. (Approved for incorporation into JP 1-02.)

multinational doctrine. The agreed upon fundamental principles that guide the employment of forces of two or more nations in coordinated action toward a common objective. (Approved for incorporation into JP 1-02.)

multinational exercise. None. (Approved for removal from JP 1-02.)

multinational force commander. A general term applied to a commander who exercises command authority over a military force composed of elements from two or more nations. Also called **MNFC.** (Approved for incorporation into JP 1-02.)

multinational operations. A collective term to describe military actions conducted by forces of two or more nations, usually undertaken within the structure of a coalition or alliance. (JP 1-02. SOURCE: JP 3-16)

multinational staff. A staff composed of personnel of two or more nations within the structure of a coalition or alliance. (Approved for incorporation into JP 1-02 with JP 3-16 as the source JP.)

rationalization. Any action that increases the effectiveness of allied forces through more efficient or effective use of defense resources committed to the alliance. (Approved for incorporation into JP 1-02.)

specialization. An arrangement within an alliance wherein a member or group of members most suited by virtue of technical skills, location, or other qualifications assume(s) greater responsibility for a specific task or significant portion thereof for one or more other members. (Approved for incorporation into JP 1-02 with JP 3-16 as the source JP.)

status-of-forces agreement. A bilateral or multilateral agreement that defines the legal position of a visiting military force deployed in the territory of a friendly state. Also called **SOFA.** (Approved for incorporation into JP 1-02.)

JOINT DOCTRINE PUBLICATIONS HIERARCHY

JP 1
JOINT DOCTRINE
JP 1-0
PERSONNEL
JP 2-0
INTELLIGENCE
JP 3-0
OPERATIONS
JP 4-0
LOGISTICS
JP 5-0
PLANS
JP 6-0
COMMUNICATIONS SYSTEM

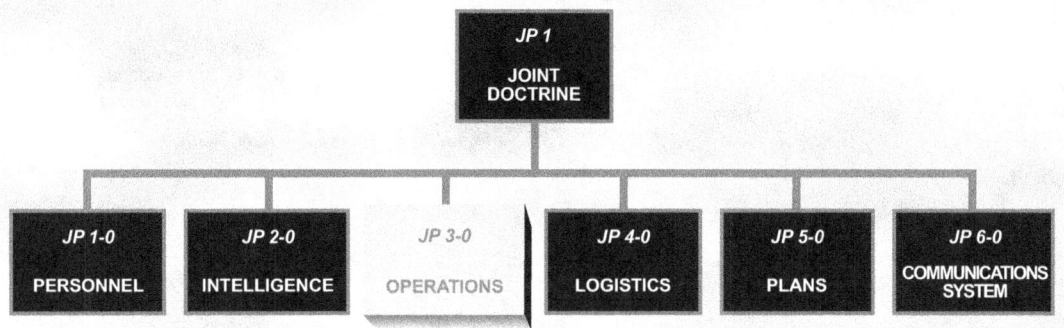

All joint publications are organized into a comprehensive hierarchy as shown in the chart above. **Joint Publication (JP) 3-16** is in the **Operations** series of joint doctrine publications. The diagram below illustrates an overview of the development process:

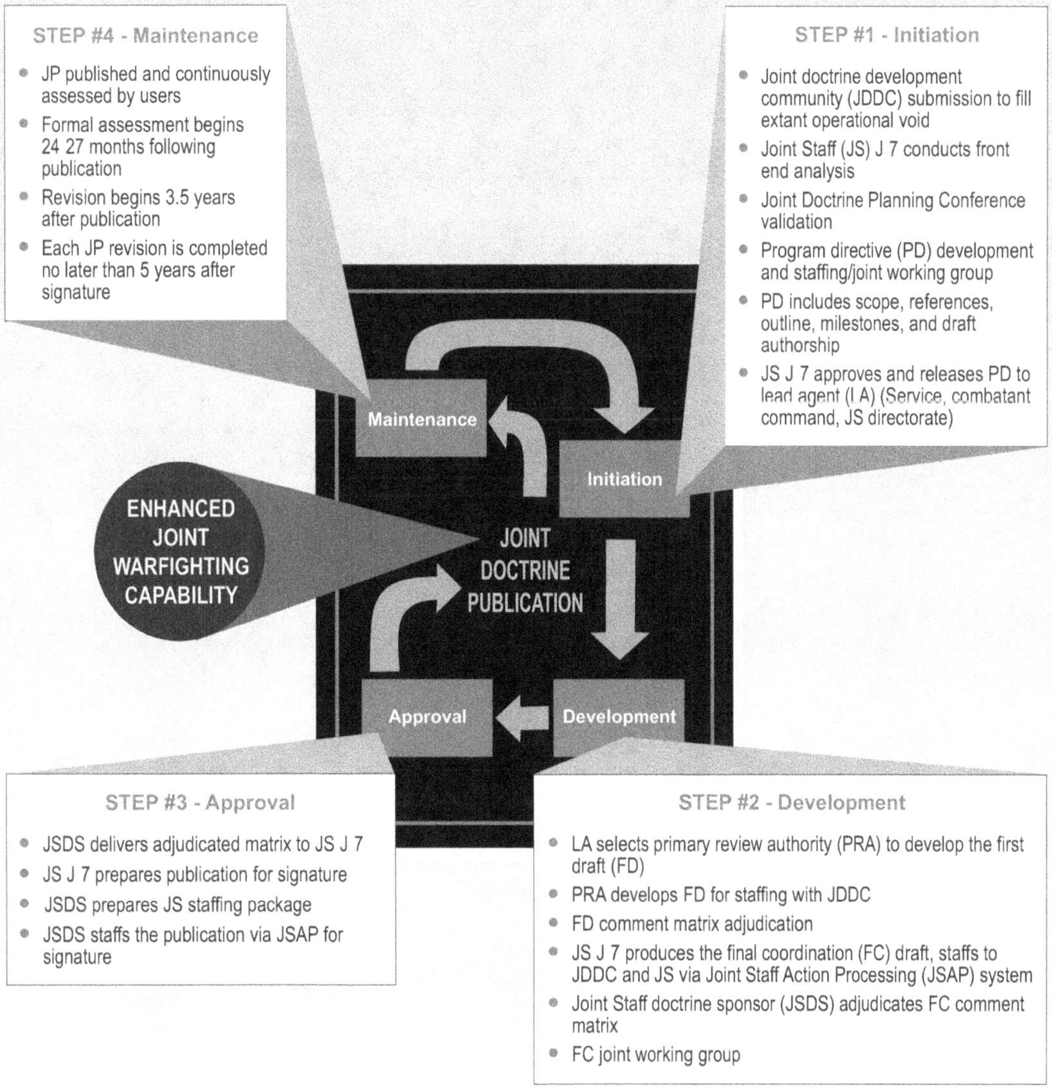

STEP #4 - Maintenance
JP published and continuously assessed by users
Formal assessment begins 24 27 months following publication
Revision begins 3.5 years after publication
Each JP revision is completed no later than 5 years after signature
STEP #1 - Initiation
Joint doctrine development community (JDDC) submission to fill extant operational void
Joint Staff (JS) J 7 conducts front end analysis
Joint Doctrine Planning Conference validation
Program directive (PD) development and staffing/joint working group
PD includes scope, references, outline, milestones, and draft authorship
JS J 7 approves and releases PD to lead agent (LA) (Service, combatant command, JS directorate)
Maintenance
Initiation
ENHANCED JOINT WARFIGHTING CAPABILITY
JOINT DOCTRINE PUBLICATION
Approval
Development
STEP #3 - Approval
JSDS delivers adjudicated matrix to JS J 7
JS J 7 prepares publication for signature
JSDS prepares JS staffing package
JSDS staffs the publication via JSAP for signature
STEP #2 - Development
LA selects primary review authority (PRA) to develop the first draft (FD)
PRA develops FD for staffing with JDDC
FD comment matrix adjudication
JS J 7 produces the final coordination (FC) draft, staffs to JDDC and JS via Joint Staff Action Processing (JSAP) system
Joint Staff doctrine sponsor (JSDS) adjudicates FC comment matrix
FC joint working group